CW01455438

BRI
FROM
THE WELL

Northern Tales in the Modern World

by

Dave Lee

Contents

Published by
Mandrake of Oxford
PO Box 250
OXFORD
OX1 1AP (UK)

A CIP catalogue record for this book is available from
the British Library and the US Library of Congress.

Introduction: The Well

Modern people commonly have a notion of time as a line, from past (usually on the left or behind us) to future (usually imagined as in front or to the right). The substance of the past is gone, emptied out, giving way to a future that doesn't exist yet. Only the slender, hurtling present is real.

There's a beguiling simplicity to this image, but it doesn't stand up to close scrutiny. Both time and the memories which lend it apparent substance are more slippery than we like to think.

It appears that the brain mechanisms we use to retrieve and relive memories of ourselves serve as the basis of future thought too. We fill our imagined future with remembered visuals, body movements and emotions. Our future is imagined using the raw materials of the past.

The past is also more complex than that, examined more closely. Memory itself is not some archive of photographs which only change by fading with time, or of audiotapes that gradually blur to static, which we re-access in their slightly-more faded realness every time we recall an experience. Far from it – it seems that each time we recall a memory we lay down a memory of recalling that memory. What we are recalling is not a faded photograph but a palimpsest, multiple views of the original event and its subsequent recallings, layered until the original memory is probably invisible under the overlays.

That palimpsest and our relation to it is better understood as the development of a narrative rather than the serial accessing of the same memory.

So it seems that we change and develop 'the past' with narrative, and we create 'the future' by re-mixing the stored elements of that narrative in order to continue it onwards. Our past lives on in our present time too, with old imprints and memories colouring and shaping our present reality. All the verbal tenses cluster around the same mighty place, the same source of narrative and mythic significance.

The ancient Germanic people had a name for this place: the Well of Urdhr. Urdhr, an Old Norse cognate of the Anglo-Saxon term *wyrd*, is one of the three Norns of fate, Urdhr, Verdhandi and Skuld, who cluster around the Well. These Norns are mighty beings, beyond and above the gods, in the sense that they are eternal and know the fates, the rise and fall, of the gods themselves. They operate at a level some call the transpersonal. They are watchers of the Well and helpers to the Tree. Everything comes from the Well, all the past and future. The Tree, which contains all the worlds in present time, all the branches of the Now, is nourished at its roots by the Well's waters.*

Knowledge of the past is attenuated in this present culture. Adverts tell us to 'make the most of now' by brain-gorging on yet more trivial data until our normal condition is of neural overload. We have no time for tales that might inspire us with values beyond mere acquisition of more consumer junk. Our collective sense of history is degraded and getting worse. Our Well is polluted with trivial nonsense that's completely irrelevant to our survival and fulfilment and is not designed to inspire noble or exceptional behaviour. Some of those who find this situation intolerable seek and sometimes find narratives that inspire them to take steps into a realm of magic and significance, where thoughts and actions count for something.

---

* Even the Germanic languages reflect this delicate distinction. English, for instance, has no proper conjugation for the future tense, but compound forms like 'I will go' or 'I'm going soon'. The philosophical implications of this idea of time are explored in depth in Paul Bauschatz's 'The Well and the Tree' [1982].

Mimir's Well
© 2004 Robert N. Taylor, *wulfing1@aol.com.*

This book consists of themes whose gleam caught my eye when I drew them up from the Well of Northern tales. It is made up of thirteen pieces – stories, essays, and a poem. Some take up themes from a specific tale and some from broader issues in the context of a renaissance of ideas from Northern tradition.

The first four pieces revolve around the beginnings of the world and the deals struck between the various races of beings near the beginning: origins of the world, the arrival of the Vanic Goddess in Asgard, and the betrothal of a Van to a Giant.

The next four pieces are about society, and the magician in or against it: the Right and Left Hand Paths; Loki and Rig.

The ninth and tenth chapters are about endings: the Ragnarok.

The final sections are an exposition of some practical magical tools derived from the Northern tradition, a rune-poem modeled on the Elder Futhark and a concluding piece that frames the whole book.

I hope to convey some of the thrill I get out of understanding our Eddic tales in terms of my own life and daily experience, in terms of a world I know. If anyone is fired up to go back to the Eddas and sagas and read with fresh eyes until these myths come to life in your flesh, and thread, bright as stars, through your strongest magics and sweetest ecstasies, then I will have succeeded.

Note about Old Norse spelling

In the face of multiple versions of spellings of Old Norse words, I make no attempt at consistency.

Chapter 1
Creation?

Creation or Evolution?

The tale we read in *Völuspá* and *Gylfaginning* of the formation of the world from cosmic fire and ice, the growth of the giant and the cow and the sacrifice of the giant to pave the way for an intelligible cosmos is not really a creation myth. There is no overall creator, sitting in gaseous solitude until he ejects everything. Rather, it is a myth about how automatic cosmic processes give rise, by a process of fatal inevitability, to stages of evolution. It provides a sophisticated hierarchy of the development of new forms. We start with cosmic principles – fire and ice, and the pregnant magical void *ginnungagap* which separates them. The next level of organization to arise is that of the androgyne Ymir and the cow Audhumla. From Ymir grows the race of giants. Among these giants are the *etins*, wise immortals who appear to us a little like the laws of the universe[1]. In parallel, Audhumla licks and shapes the matrix of ice and salt where a proto-man is growing. These new forms interbreed to form the first truly conscious beings – Odin and his two brothers Vili and Ve. The brothers dismember Ymir, the old universe, and build a new one which reflects their conscious state. Consciousness is carried forward from the gods into the stream of organic life when the three brothers endow two trees with that spark and give rise to the first man and woman.

This story can engage in a fruitful dialogue with our best modern ideas of how everything arose, unlike the perverse notion of creation by a god from outside the process of the world. We can see that we are living in a layered universe, each layer of novel development stacked on top of another layer of completed development, like Koestler's concept of *holons*[2]. All the structures that our awareness is built on top of are still visible. All the ancient layers are still with us.

Philosophical ideas of evolution existed before Darwin applied the idea to the development of organic life. The founder of Neoplatonism, Plotinus, declared that the Absolute emanated increasingly dense and imperfect entities until we reached the utmost density in material forms. This concept of the 'great chain of being' formed a backdrop to Western thought for centuries, and thinkers[3] in the 20th century pointed out that the great chain had become 'temporalized', maybe at some point in the eighteenth century. Against such an intellectual background, Lamarck speculated that biological forms evolve, and subsequently Darwin suggested a believable mechanism for that evolution.

Some modern evolutionists are aware of the intellectual parenthood of the idea. As Sean Nee[4] expresses it:

> Common presentations of evolution mirror the great chain by viewing the process as progressive. For example, in their book THE MAJOR TRANSITIONS IN EVOLUTION, John Maynard Smith and Eors Szathmáry take us from the origin of life, through to the origin of eukaryotic cells, multicellularity, human societies and, finally, of language.

Instead of emanation from a perfect source, we now have evolution towards greater complexity, subtlety and refinement of structure. The ideas are not the same, but they do seem to be strongly related, in an inverse way: Plotinus's emanations descend from rarefied to dense, and organic evolution proceeds 'upwards' from simple to complex. Looking back along the line of evolution of matter and life, we move from the complex world we live in to a world that displays fewer, more universal powers and beings. With a myth of beginnings, we are seeking back to our source.

Let's invent a minimalist myth of origins: Primordial consciousness arises in the roaring, churning continuum of the forest. It divides and knows it is separate, isolate. Then it knows it is going to die, that its death is already written, scripted in the flesh. Everything else is a filling-in of the details.

Our stories of the gods are signposts to the numinous, to higher states and stages of awareness. An origin myth tells us how we got here – with a reverse striptease in which naked primordial consciousness becomes clothed in the patterns of the familiar world, via some particular, special number of veilings of that nakedness. In the Northern stories, that special number is often nine.

I have hung the tales and ideas in this essay onto that robust old story, understood as a sequence of nine stages.

The Beings of the Worlds

Today we have reached a stage where our knowledge is a dismembered supergiant, each blood-drenched fragment competing with all the others. We need stories that make sense of these fragmented voices, that weave very different viewpoints into a coherent picture of the human world.

The different dimensions of our experience can be voiced by the races of beings in the Northern tales. I have tried to give voice to the various entities that occupy the world, and who might tell a origin tale from their own viewpoints.

Dwarves we can find: they labour still, in the secret places of the body and mind, because they are the forces of habit, the ingrained things that actually work well, and so go on working, without anyone needing to interfere in their craft. On one level, they represent biology. In another sense, they

11

can be seen as the skills that underlie our action in the world. I present a magical system of working with this concept in Chapter 11.

In yet another sense, they comprise the face of our consciousness that is ever pointed outwards towards matter; what transpersonal researcher Stanislav Grof labels *hylotropic* consciousness, as distinct from the inward-directed *holotropic* awareness. Dwarves forge the details of our sensory world.

The etins or wise giants also make up our external, objective world, but they are a more remote and alien aspect of nature than the dwarves. They speak for the vast, inhuman systems that are the customs of the physical universe. They speak for the inside of matter, matter on its own terms. They are allied to physics and systems theory.

In vision: *Now we are on a metal road, with sides curving up. My horse has steel armour, may be a steel horse now. The road becomes a bridge over starry space, with massive shadowy presences about us (we are too little to attract much attention). I realise we are in a realm of total illusion (like Thor & Loki in Utgard). We are in something like cyberspace. This is the realm of mineral forces, quartz crystals in passage graves, quartz crystals in electronic equipment, providing the interior world of cyberspace through etinic agency...*

...in the distance, Etinhome is a pimple of mountain on the horizon. I ride towards it. Close up it is not a mountain, but an arrangement of mirrors, reflecting automatic industrial processes, no people of any kind, like an abandoned factory that's still producing.

The etins remind me of Gregory Bateson's concept of Mind At Large. He illustrates this with the way a forest after a fire will repair itself in a certain ecological sequence. He calls this 'intelligence', and distinguishes it from human awareness, which he calls 'consciousness', and which he regards as a very limited form of Mind At Large, the forest intelligence. This position is of a piece with the fact that

Bateson was one of the original theoreticians of computing back in the nineteen forties.

Bateson's model seems to see us as essentially the same as giants, just as Extropians believe we will one day upload ourselves into computers instead of dying. Such radical reductionists of consciousness argue the position of computer theoretician Alan Turing's infamous Test: that we have no more subjectivity than a computer program of equal complexity to our own processes. Do I believe that? No. My position on this issue may be summed up as: Don't be taken in by etinbollocks.

In general, cosmologies and philosophies that seek to 'transcend' – or should we say, more honestly, to sidestep or deny? – the problems and pains of being human - or even humanity itself - by reference to cosmological stuff, impressing us with how symmetrical some enormous model is – are etinic, giantish. Most forms of Theosophy and its descendants are shot through with such thinking.

Giants and bureaucracy mix well – anything that is dehumanizing in a rational, ever-so-well-meaning way reeks of etinbollocks. We might imagine etin accountants who balance the loss of lives, with a numerical weighting for different degrees of sentience.

Another feature of our relationship with giants is in the straight, terrain-oblivious lines, sighting lines underlined in track and stone, we find the world over. In Northern Europe some of these roads are only ever used for funeral processions – the so-called death roads. In straight lines, death and stone we see the tracks of the giants.

Elves also speak for our relationship with the natural world – but in this instance through the medium of the human imagination. William Blake reminded us that the imagination is the most spiritual of our intellectual qualities, and the elves speak for the ascent of human consciousness to the experience of 'nature mysticism', the vivid sense of identity with the entire natural world. Their realm is, on one level, the arts.

The gods - Aesir and Vanir - are the voices of both our subjectivity and of culture, both our inward spiritual quest and our ways of encoding it in religions. The gods bring about links, divine marriages, between different races of beings. We read of the giving of consciousness to humans by Odin, Vili and Ve, tying us into the conscious world. Odin also ensouls the dwarves, from the maggots in Ymir's flesh.

The origin tale in *Völuspá* is told by the *volva* or seeress whom Odin has roused for this purpose. So who is she? A giant? Only giants are older than the god who goes to her for the story. But really; is she not too human…?

I shall return to this question.

Preamble, Or Act 0: The Seeress

She sits in a cave at the centre of all edges, in the twilight of morning, in the red dusk behind closed eyes. In her gaze the universe around her creates and destroys, harvests and sows, cherishes and abandons, emits and absorbs, spins the moon's emptiness and fullness…

The soundtrack is a timeless music, as if you just walked into a performance that has been going on for forty thousand years. Serpent time: broken, jerky rhythms that coalesce into the spinning infinity of deep trance.

Where she sits is the heart of a crystal that is all of space, three axes meeting here at the centre of everything, a singular point alight with windows onto all the worlds.

A single eye blazes out from under the traveller's broad-brimmed hat. He leans forward. 'So how did it begin?'

She takes a long silent breath. Her eyeballs roll up under closed eyelids, as if she is brimming with something.

'It happened in stages. Each stage led to the next, with no possibility of it happening any other way.'

This was the first of aeons, when Ymer built.
There was no soil, no sea, no waves;
Earth was not, nor heaven;
Gaping abyss alone: no growth.
Sun knew not what hall she had;
Stars knew not their places yet.
Moon knew not his power.

Act 1: Fire And Ice

In the polarity of cosmic Ice and Fire arises the spring Hvergelmir, rivers of venom roll, frost fills the gap, thaws and drips...

We are in a moment before life appears, in the presence of the most primal layer of power.

Voice of a giant: In all your highest art you are in awe of the silence of mountains and stars. Our customs are the genetics of the universe. See here *Blaínn*, the Black One, whom you call space. See here *Brimir* - the earliest of all Laws, of whom all you know now is the echo of his roar, the background radiation in emptiness.

We are the sacred memories of inanimate matter itself. We are the original narrators. We're as cosmic as it gets.

Voice of a dwarf: Well, Fire and Ice is all very well, and not a word of untruth - but you really should hear the details. I wouldn't want you to go away with the impression that it all starts out nice and neat, with straight lines and sacred geometries and all that stuff. That's etinbollocks, and comes a lot later. You see, the Ginnung, the magical substance of Ginnungagap is frothy, foamy, and bubbles form randomly at the interface of the fire and ice. The smaller ones are naturally attracted more strongly towards the ice than the big ones –

thus the different sizes sort themselves out, like sand sifting through gravel which in turn sifts through pebbles. As they are squashed by the increasing pressure of the bubbles above them, they form lattices - invariably hexagonal, with the exotic six-fold symmetries of snowflakes. These give rise to the first crystal-like formations on the surface of the ice. Thus three dimensional geometry, with its straight lines, comes into being. And salt.

Voice of an elf: I never thought I'd agree with a dwarf. Yes – in the beginning a bubblebud formed from a wound in an older universe, and there were bubbles, big, fat glistening bubbles. They each epibubbled and formed bubbles-within-bubbles. There came many bubbles within bubbles, until all space (which was small, or the bubbles were very big) was filled with them.

A pattern formed: Only certain, particular numbers of bubbles of a particular fractional size could be contained within one greater bubble, and so these ratios prospered and stabilized. And so, notionally joining the centres of the bubbles together, we got imaginary straight lines. It was the thin end of the wedge; the circle never was squared but the sphere was hexed and pented, giving birth in no time to cubes, icosahedrons and all that straight-edge stuff. So that's how it happened, venom and all.

Act 2: The Cow And The Androgyne

He lives on the melting ice, always has done. In the frost-covered void he meets the cow Audhumla and feeds from the streams of milk that flow from her four udders. She too is always there, a child of the Gap-frost. She smells salt and moves away from the hot place. She blends into the mist, through which occasionally emerge glimpses of an icy void, her world ending just over *there*. She follows the bloody scent to the edge of the ice sheet. She lives on an eternal edge, on a shrunken border between two unlivable extremes, two universes of death. The air is always wet.

Act 3: The Giants

Ymir inherited the fertility of the Gap in a different way to her. Sucking in its vast free lunch, he lived and prospered, a sublime, grotesque, unconscious, automatistic perfection. His organs mated as he slept and sweated, slept in a lumpy void with no particular up or down, slept with a Möbius strip as a pillow.

Ymir, the sloppy, dirty supergiant, already his parts have fucked, one with another, and bred giants. Each of his brood, stemming as it did from a burned-out completeness, a husk of an old flower gone to seed, took with it part of his form and power and wandered off to do giant things.

Act 4: The First Mind

Audhumla lay down in the dim red light, licking her way further into the wall of cosmic ice. The third being came as no surprise for her. Cows are not equipped for surprise, and when a half-grown, unthreatening life form appeared in the ice she just kept on licking. It grew towards her warmth, her udders swelled with expectation, and she mooed softly in pleasure at this Other to love and nurture. It looked like a man.

And the man-being bred with a giant, and the universe's etin-genetics reshuffled once again – giving rise to Odin.

Maybe that, then, is why Ymir, the unconscious universe, went to sleep: because consciousness had arrived. Odin immediately gets a grip on the situation and out of the pre-conscious chaos slumbering around him he hacks a meaningful world.

Act 5: Time Begins With A Murder

Ymir is a grimy slob, his beer belly hanging over the edge of the greasy settee where he has snoozed for millennia, one leg fucking with the other, entities crawling out of his armpits. This is the dregs of a previous cycle of time, of evolution, as witnessed by the new stage – consciousness, Odin.

Odin walks in, and with aristocratic contempt, says 'Look at this fucking mess', and proceeds to make a universe from Ymir's body and blood and hair, his empty plastic takeaway containers, cans and fag ends, the leavings of that former perfection.

It is a triumph of consciousness, not because the pre-conscious, Ymir, is evil – but because that is what consciousness *has* to do – that is what this tale tells us: Undifferentiated unity must be broken for individual consciousness to arise. Or, *time begins with a murder.*

Now the TV is on a dead channel, the 3.5 Kelvin background grime of the cosmos fizzing on a grainy screen. The eruption came and went and still just crackles on as new awarenesses gape with awe at its incredible velocity and ferocious meaninglessness. That is what it's like at the beginning of time.

Act 6: Subcontract, Automate, Devolve Power: The Dwarves

The orderly dwarves built the hierarchies within which they live, built the whole world of perception, opened the eyes of the world... and eventually united with its light and life, when the Lady came to love them; but that is another tale, for another time.

You can find the secret powers, still at work in the world...

There's this cave, see, and in order to get inside it, you have to become very small, like the people who are already in there. And when you do become small, you find that you have become like the people inside, and you start to remember… to remember who really made everything… and so absorbed in your work are you, that you never even talk about it, not for tens of thousands of years … when tea-break finally happens … And then you're not supposed to talk about anything important … but everybody does. And that's when you learn how many different beings think they run this universe…

Who should fashion a host of dwarfs
From Brimer's blood and the limbs of the dead?

Voice of dwarf: Yes - Who foots the bill? Who's running the show? You see, the giants would like everyone to think it's them. OK, the etins did get the spacetime franchise, and so that makes all the really impressive physical constants like the proton-electron mass-ratio and the Hubble number etin genetics, so they snoot around as if they owned spacetime and everything in it. But, as everyone knows, they had to cut a deal over particles with the elven folks. We dark-elves got the dense, impenetrable fermions, all the stuff you make gold and diamonds with. (The fermions actually appeared via wormholes when the original nine dimensions crashed down into four, hence the dark-elf association with maggots.) The light-elves got the soft friendly bosons, the electromagnetic spectrum - light itself. And some say that humans may well end up living there in Andlang, living in boson substrates instead of flesh…

Let me tell you about the dwarves and the organic world: Apprentices usually start with worms. These are very simple for the nimble dwarf fingers – a mere tube of mud hollowed out, and then inverted, turned around inside itself, whilst the sacred word is whispered. This is, of course, *fee fi fo fum.*

Anyway, I digress. The nice jobs are doing the clouds and suchlike. The giants get a lot of that work – mackerel sky in fractal folds, tooled by a windy bunch of puffing-billy elementals, great haughty dangerous etins with a deceptive ease and sweetness about them. Mackerels themselves are of course the province of another department, the lavishly-funded Vertebrate Phylum.

I digress again. The point is, we are left in the back room now, just making things. Nice things, though.

Act 7: The Gift Of Self To Self

Consciousness has arrived. The god has acted; what does it mean? He is alone in a universe that he has set in motion. He will wrest meaning from it by an act of sacrifice, in order to interact with the only other thing he can possibly interact with: the totality, all that he is not: the cosmos.

So, Odin met the Other, and gained the runes. And what is it he gained, what is a futhark? That the runes represent the peak of learning in both secular and sacred realms is indicated by this passage in *Rigsthula:*

> But King, young Kon the youngest boy alone knew runes, runes eternal and runes of life, ageless runes, and runes of mystery. He knew how to help in childbirth, deaden sword-blades, quiet the ocean. He understood birds' speech, quenched fires, pacified and quietened men, made sorrows disappear, had the strength and vigour of eight men.

Futhark is a highest-level map; what magical writer Peter Carroll calls a psychocosm. Everything that was known at the time could be hung onto its structure. And not only that, but the futhark would have enriched the man of that time's understanding of the relationships between those elements of knowledge, the staves of the rune-row.

Also, a rune row may be something like a time capsule, a telegraphic compression of cultural myth, values, aspirations, lore and law, disguised as an alphabet. Like a computer virus hidden in the code of an innocuous-looking file, its message remains inviolable for athelings to read in some unknown future.

We can still do that, map anything and everything we can think of onto the staves of the Elder rune-row, but we have to use it cunningly to reflect the shifting horizons of this Wolf-Age.

Our mysteries were encoded in other forms before the futhark, and may yet be encoded in some new, undreamt of form.

Act 8: And Here We Are!

The god has encoded the keys to consciousness in the runes. Now this pattern must be passed on to other sentient life.

So we come to the creation of humans, to the part of the story where we try to explain ourselves to ourselves, to understand what kind of being we are. The story of the three brothers ensouling us gives three forces, three centres, three 'brains'.

Other stories give us maps too, such as the tale of the tree Yggdrasil taken as a psychocosm of daily life: There stands in the midst of the world a tree, called Yggdrasil. It weaves from three roots a triple skein of men, giants and the dead. An eagle crowns its branches, the hawk Vedhrfolnir sitting between its piercing eyes. The tree suffers great hardships – the dragon Nidhogg gnaws at it from below, four stags devour its leaves, and the squirrel Ratatosk runs up and down the trunk bearing malicious messages between Nidhogg and the eagle. The Norns that live by the Wyrd well plaster its trunk each day with holy white mud, preserving it against these depredations.

Now might the eagle be the Self surveying its world, bothered ceaselessly by the self-talk, the internal dialogue which is Ratatosk, bearing the unwelcome wisdom of Nidhogg? Nidhogg's message, that gnaws at the root of identity, is the awareness of our own mortality. And might the gnawing stags be the little losses and defeats as death eats away at our daily life? Against this daily attrition we must work as best we can by daily communion with sacredness, with vital power. Our daily discipline raises up sacred brightness to anoint our mundane lives.

Now the Hawk we can understand as the ever-present witness, what English mage Austin Spare called the Kia or atmospheric I, the observing Self he glyphed as a vulture, hovering over the feast of life and death. Further, the falcon or hawk is the beast-vehicle of goddesses Frigg and Freyja as seeresses. Maybe we have here the identity of the Seeress whom Odin consults in the beginning – his priestess-wife or lover.

Act 9: Deals, Ends, Beginnings

The realm of the gods is established, and now the Aesir, the tribe of Odin, the gods of conscious life, enter into relationships with the other entities that inhabit their universe. However, the deals they make are subject to the laws of that universe, its ancient layers, and the seeds of its downfall are sown at the same moments as many of the actions that create and sustain that world. As Edred Thorsson expresses it:

The new cosmos of Wodhanaz-Wiljon-Wihaz[5] cannot avoid its own dissolution (as neither could that of the Ymir). However, the cosmos of Wodhanaz-Wiljon-

Wihaz has within it the ability to transcend its own mortality and reconstitute itself beyond the limits of its own demise. This is reflected in the story of how the world regenerates itself after the final stage of Ragnarok. [6]

The Ragnarok is the tale of the completion of the processes of creation, the return of the cycle to its origin-point, the end and a new beginning.

Notes

1 Another race of giants also appears in the old tales – the *thurses* are the stupid, lumbering brutes of ogre stories, not usually represented as possessing the terrifying inhuman intelligence of the etins.
2 Arthur Koestler expounded the notion of the holon in "The Ghost in the Machine" (1967). A holon has two faces: an assemblage of parts but also a complete entity that acts in itself as part of greater whole. An atom is made of smaller particles, and whole atoms assemble into molecules, which form parts of cells, and so on up the chain of structures.
3 See Arthur O. Lovejoy's *The Great Chain of Being*, 1936.
4 Sean Nee, *Nature* 2005 435:429
5 The Old Germanic form of Odin-Vili-Ve
6 Edred Thorsson, Rune Gild communication, 2007

Chapter 2 The Joining of the Races

Having sculpted an entire cosmos out of an older layer of being, the Aesir, the gods of Odin's kin, come to discover by stages the other powerful beings and even gods who inhabit the worlds adjacent to theirs. In *Völuspá* 8 the Aesir are seen happily playing, then suddenly being interrupted in their innocent ease:

They played tables in the garth and were blissful.
None of them lacked gold, until three maidens
came from the Thurses. Their might was awesome,
they came from Ettinhome. [1]

A new power has arrived, and this interruption in the gods' bliss is the signal to create the dwarves and then to ensoul the first human beings from a pair of trees. Then the forces of fate, the Norns, put in an appearance:

I know an ash that stands, called Yggdrasil,
a tall tree, wet with white dews,
dews dripping down into the dales.
Ever green it stands over Urth's well.
From there come three maidens, deep in lore,
from the water that stands under the tree.
One is called Urth, the other Verthandi,
the third Skuld. Scores they carved,
laws they laid, lives they chose.
They worked Orlog for the sons of men.

Asgard is now completed with its defensive walls, but the Aesir are not to be left in peace. The next arrival is a woman, a goddess, who is a stirrer of strife. Gullveig ('Gold-Drunkenness' or 'Power of Gold') is stabbed and burned three times, but arises whole from the flames. Now she is Heith ('Fame' or 'Shining'), a name given to witches.

I recall the first battle in the world.
There they stabbed Gullveig with spears,
and burned her in Har's hall.
Thrice she was burned, thrice she was born.
It happened often, and yet she lives.
She is called Heith, who comes to houses, the far
seeing spae woman. The wise volva knew gand
magic, she understood seith. She played with minds
by her seith. She was always dear to evil women.

Here the kind of innocence that is lost is more explicit: Gullveig has brought a new kind of greed into Asgard, a greed for riches and fine things. She is implicitly the Goddess of the Vanir, and therefore identified with the deity known simply as Freyja/Freya, the Lady. Freya's daughter is Hnoss, Old Norse for treasure or jewel, said to have given her name to all precious things.

Of course, there is more than this to the Lady. Her gifts include beauty, appreciation of beauty and sensuality. At the vulgar end these gifts become greed, institutionalized as consumerism in the modern world. At the more restrained end of the scale, beauty is refined by a transcendent influence. This is the realm of aesthetics, of beauty made manifest – first in desirable flesh, in the beauty of a beloved face, then in art via craft, the agency of the Dwarves, the skilled ones who forge beautiful things.

In the Gullveig story, the goddess shows a face of primal greed for pleasure. Her primal appetites are then subjected to spears and fire – the pointed gaze of the transcendent, and

25

the heat of furious concentration – resulting in a transmutation into ecstasy, in which she shines.

Sensuality has collided with transcendence, in a powerful moment of refinement. Sex, for instance, can be enjoyed as satisfaction of gross appetite, or transmuted, refined into ecstasy. Sensuality transcends into music, song, art. The Lady too is changed by the encounter, and when she comes to live in Asgard, she is married to Odhr, a name that seems to mean 'Ecstasy'. Freya weeps tears of gold at his prolonged absence. She has come to love the ecstasy born of transcendence, of the refinement of appetites, of the transmutation of fleshly pleasure.

The outlines of the Vanic goddess are obscured by time and christianity's destruction of the Vanic ways, the aboriginal earth-magic, a cultural layer even more at odds with monotheism than was the worship of the Aesir. Even her name is difficult to pin down – in the layer of history we have access to, she is known only as the Lady, Freya, a root commonplace enough to pass into modern German as Frau. Her older names, we can only guess at. Beauty, art and sexual ecstasy are seen in this face of the Lady, as are greed and intoxication. The name Gullveig seems to resonate with the old Irish goddess-name Maedb, meaning 'the intoxicated one'. Is it, then, acquisitiveness that stirs the Aesir to attack her, in a confrontation as violent as a cosmic thunderstorm, between sky-gods and a goddess of the earth and the flesh, or is it her drunken laughter?

They pierce and burn her, but she shines. She is outside of the law of the Aesir, and her power is one of the great powers of the world and therefore indestructible, so they cannot vanquish it but have to come to terms with it. Not before having a war, though. *Völuspá* 23:

Then all the Regin went to the doom chair.

The Ginn Holy Gods held moot
as to whether the Aesir should pay tribute
or whether all the gods should have a wassail.
Odin sped a shot into the host.
That was the first battle in the world.
The board wall was broken, the fortification
of the Ases. The fighting Vanes trod the battlefield

The war between the Aesir and the Vanir leads by a kind of dialectic to a third being, created from the spit of the two races of gods and wiser than either race – Kvasir[2]. Kvasir is converted by murder and art into a mead that brings wisdom and poetry. Odin's theft of this precious substance, the Stirrer of Inspiration, is a wild, shamanic tale of travel, shape-shifting and deceit.

In the wake of the war, three of the Van come to live in Asgard as hostages, Njordh, Freya and Frey. They are accepted into the home of the Aesir, Odin giving Frey (the Lord) the realm of Alfheim as a 'tooth-gift'. This suggests the Vanic god came to live amongst the Aesir as a young child, in the tradition of sending aristocratic children to (often distant) relatives to further their education and cement bonds between branches of the clan. Frey is a hostage, but an honoured one.

The gift of Alfheim, the world of the elves, is significant – Frey is probably identical with the old earth-god Ing/Ingwaz, and therefore better suited to liaise with the elven folk than one of the Aesir.

This is the first joining of the races of the worlds. In *Skirnismal*, the next link appears – the Vanic god Frey is married to a giant, Gerdh.

Frey finds Odin's high seat unoccupied and sits in it. From that place of vision, he sees into the world of the etins, the wise giants, sees a golden hall and a beautiful woman. It seems his love for her is hopeless, because gods are forbidden to marry giants. Or so Frey thinks, in his despair. His messenger Skirnir ('Shining One') saves him by offering to bring Gerdh home to marry Frey. Skirnir achieves this with his last resort, threatening rune magic against her.

It appears that Odin sets up the whole situation – he vacates his high seat, so that Frey can fall in love and bring about the changes. Odin also provides an attempted betrothal gift, the ring Draupnir that multiples itself every ninth night, though it is rejected by Frey's alien beloved. Odin does this, even though Frey's intended belongs to the forbidden race of etins. This tribal transgression, this bit of cosmic exogamy, is the final link that ties together the races of Aesir, Vanir and giants, the elves already being tied into the Vanir by Odin's 'tooth-gift' to Frey of Alfheim.

The story of Frey and Gerdh has some odd resonances with modern humans' relationship to information technology. Gerdh may be likened to the completely alien mineral consciousness of silicon – bright and shining in the eastern sun, cold and white, atomically similar to carbon – why doesn't it make life like carbon does? But it does – etin life, that cannot find wisdom in the *Hávamál*, that has no lust for fruits, for immortality, for gold, for anything a carbon-based life-form would recognize as useful or fun. It's getting on with its own slow timestream, away from ours, and it's happy that way. Only brute force of magical will in a moment of desperation works, to bring it into the realm of the other races, to marry it with the Lord of Life, to create a new form of life.

Was this mineral consciousness originally an echo of the quartz chambers of the Neolithic passage graves? Frey, the Lord of Nature rules these, and there is a sense in which their function is to transmute humans into the elven stream via interaction with silica substrates over long periods of time, an alchemical marriage of dead human, crystalline, etinic stone and elven nature. In this century, of course, the world half-expects the fast but stupid silicon-based computer to evolve soon into a true intelligence, or something very like it. It is almost as if the great bard who first told *Skirnismal* programmed the intellectual preconditions for the manifestation of mineral intelligence centuries later. In that version, Skirnir is the technician, the scientist, who makes the damn thing work, who has to do the dirty work of cursing dumb silicon into reluctant life, presenting this new being as a *fait accompli* to his master.

Notes

1   All Edda quotes from James Chisholm, *Edda*
2   The resemblance of the name Kvasir to those of drinks (Russian *kvass* etc) is unlikely to be a mere coincidence. Spitting into a ferment is one way to get it started.

Chapter 3
Shining Fear

Seeking a beginning, she has never got past her vision of the end. In that vision, it is always bright moonlight, a frozen howl in the spine. White sticks like bleached bones in the forest clearing, by a ruined wall. Two bodies crouch in shadow, one squats in moon dapple. That one raises a blade of bland silver light and opens the edge of her palm to let the blackness well out.

She knows this scene, and aches to see what comes before it. She rewinds the vision, running the images backwards like a familiar reel of film, a film that always breaks just as she glimpses the hilltop house, the castle of the magician.

This time is different. Her concentration is pure, her heart still and serene in the chaos. When the tall stone house with its mansard roof and mullioned windows appears, it is solid enough to walk into, so, in the enclosing night she steps up onto the porch and pushes the heavy, dark door open. She just has time to register a pale something flying at her face, which she hurls a pentagram at. Her banishing doesn't entirely work, and she knows it's time to turn and run.

She doesn't turn back again until she is down the slope of the drive, then looks round to see a pale vortex in the black air. By a supreme act of will, she pushes it away and runs, but the servitor is still there, like a jagged shard of TV screen in the corner of her eye. Out, now, get out!

She did the necessary magical cleansing, once she'd finished being sick. She rubbed the fear-sweat back into her skin and composed herself for meditation, the trembling dying down. An hour later, the spirit had gone, leaving only a taste of hungry violence. She showered and slept.

They would be in touch, of that she was certain.

*

A tall, athletic redhead is smoking a Marlboro on a flagged patio one floor above the city's traffic roar. The excited, attentive set of her eyes and mouth leak her adoration of London, its noise and buzz and in-yer-face enforced contact.

A few corporate yards away, the phone rings for her. The security camera's all-seeing eye gulps radians of the half-indoor brandscape: bonsai shrubs, bulbous post-industrial furniture, blue perspex conduits ducting overhead streams of water. The shock-haired skinny receptionist takes the call. Pop stick of chewing gum, lose twenty IQ points.

The message routes to Jade's phone just as she walks back in. It's a good omen for a quest, for a midsummer weekend that will change her life. She takes up the phone, her voice breathy and hopeful. 'Hello?'

'Good morning Jade' It was the lush, sexy voice of her new friend Maire, the dark, intense woman who'd turned up in her life the day after her vision-quest, stunning and elegant in the Thai buffet where she was eating lunch.

Her breath was coming fast and she focused carefully, because Maire was inviting her to a party, not just any party, but the intro she'd been waiting for, her passport to a bigger and more magical world.

'These people are the real deal', said Maire, 'the full-time magical elite. You won't recognize any of them, but they run the top end of everything and they're all loaded and dangerous.'

Jade had come from the provinces, from out of another life. Her sociable, competitive spirit had opened up like a flower to London's light. She'd dived into her natural medium, the occult scene. The shallow end of that pool had entertained her to an autumn moulded by spells and sharpened by conflict.

Half of it hadn't even been her doing at all – dolls in freezers, curses hissed in crowded pub rooms, an absolute minimum of three marriages in ruins. Astonishing how little these nice people seemed to want to witness in the way of real magic, how much less they actually wanted to do. They seemed content to talk about it while they got drunk.

Her trance work, uncanny accuracy drawn from apparent delirium, had terrified them. That had convinced her that the real magical action was somewhere else, and she'd decided to apply her own magical skills to find the people of real power.

After the phone call, it was an effort to force herself back to work. So that she could feel strong, she visited her special high place, riding down from the moorlands of her childhood, back to the stables, to the smell of the hot horses and their leather, the massive beauty of the great animals soothing her as always, their very existence like strong arms around her, making her feel good and secure. Her eyes softened, she smiled a vague, inward kind of smile, and stepped back into corporate fairyland.

*

The house was up by the Heath, a warren of fantastic rooms. The downstairs was like a super-posh fetish fashion show, glittering with hot beauty, dripping with sex. Jade was at home there, easy in her power. She strutted amongst the antiques, the oil paintings and beauties, greeted, mingled and smiled, was admired, desired and hated for her power. After a while, she went exploring. There was a dungeon downstairs, where an old man was handcuffed to a rig at one end, while a strong, red-faced woman ran the length of the room to lash him with a rhino whip. She watched, fascinated by how the old skin was barely wealed by blows that would rip her flesh open, and this desperate old bastard was still crying out for more.

After a while there was nothing to do but leave these people to their delights and go on searching for the heart of the party, the dark heart that Maire had assured her would lift her breath in shock. Up, past bedrooms leaking groans and laughter, up past tiny camps of whispered intrigue, up into the gable of the house, where she found the top room.

It was very odd there. The space seemed to warp and flow as she walked in. The music was dark, overwhelmingly intense, hushed bass choirs over tortured fuzz, and someone crying, rhythmically.

Someone was laughing, too, coaxingly, dementedly, disturbingly: a voice tilted off the edge of obsession into childlike babbling.

Her eyes adjusted and she saw a dungeon lit only by candlelight, a fleshy dark girl obscured by grainy red... blood?, writhing on a cross with upswept arms. Her tormentor's broad back, rilled with bright sweat, shook with his potent glee. Against the far wall, she made out an altar, a giant slab of stone covered in objects which seemed to have an impossible amount of sentience compressed into them, spilling alien fear into the room.

On her left, a strong-built, masked man rose from a leather couch and motioned her politely to sit beside him. They were skew-wise on to the cross, and the big man turned to face her fully. She could see through the executioner's mask that he was smiling levelly as he extended his palm with a square of brightly-coloured blotting paper on it. She kept eye contact for a few breaths, then smiled and leaned forward, licking the acid from his hand. The big man seemed quietly pleased as he turned back to the sadomasochistic tableau.

She counted fifty steady breaths, watching the scene, listening to the pain-giver's curiously childlike voice, and then he turned right round to face Jade.

He grinned like a wolf, greedy privileged eyes staring out of a ruined blonde elegance. 'So what are you after, cat-girl? A bit of sacred punishment?'

Jade gazed into his black eyes, taking a couple of breaths to make a smile. 'I am greedy for power. Do you have any?'

The sadist let out a scornful, hooting laugh 'I can certainly offer cat-girl something very powerful' he leered,

He crossed to the altar and picked up a tiny scoop of black glass. He put it to his nose and sniffed noisily, then exhaled with a roaring sound, blowing white dust over the altar. He turned to Jade, his face frozen in thoughtless velocity, and proffered the spoon.

'No, thank you' Jade said softly. 'I prefer sacraments that actually make a difference'.

A flash of anger crossed the straining face, and he turned his back on Jade. He strode over to the cross, unroped one of the girl's arms, and headed for the back of the altar to an exit Jade hadn't noticed.

'Be ready at midnight, Vincius' he snapped, as he stepped out. The dark girl followed.

Jade heard footsteps going down the hidden stairs, and she turned to face the masked man.

'Thank you, Vincius' she said.

'Alex, please; we're not in Hugo's game yet'.

'And what might Hugo's game be?'

'Power! Same as yours, it seems'

'And yours is something else?'

Alex laughed.

Jade caught the glint of his eyes behind the mask and leaned towards him. 'So,' she drawled 'what happens at midnight?'

'Magical power happens, if all goes right. Salammbo will achieve a deep trance and we will ask her questions'.

'Can I join in too? I am a trance priestess'.

Alex nodded slowly 'That, and allowing Hugo to torture you, might just buy your entrance. Are you any good?'

'Generally, I frighten people. Is that good?'

'Oh yes, that's very good. I shall recommend to Hugo that you join us tonight. Meanwhile, I am going to prepare myself'. With that, Alex closed his eyes and fell silent.

Jade saw his chest rising and falling, heard a whispered mantra fade into silence. She found her own breath falling into easy rhythm with Alex's, and she stilled her mind, gazing with peripheral vision at the sumptuous temple around them. Time passed without measure, and then the music became louder and Hugo reappeared, leading the naked, blindfolded Salammbo by a silken cord that passed through a nipple piercing. Jade was beginning to find Hugo's aesthetics irritating.

Alex stood and performed a resonant, powerful chant while Hugo tied the silent girl to the cross again. Jade saw her stumble as she stepped up the tiny step. She leaned limply against her bonds. Hugo sprinkled white powder into a golden thurible and wafted it under Salammbo's nose. She jerked upright and let out a brief, babbling cry, then slumped again. Hugo turned to Alex and said 'She's not turned out to be much use, has she?'

Behind him, Salammbo was snuffling and groaning. Alex sighed, went over and untied her, supporting her onto the couch.

'So what do we do now, Vincius?' said Hugo.

'Jade here says she is a trance priestess'.

It was as if Hugo only then noticed Jade standing there. 'OK, let's see if you're any good'. He had a glazed look and was advancing, fondling a whip. 'Tie 'er up, Vincius!'

Alex said 'Rules, Hugo! Jade, which, if any, of pain, fear and humiliation don't you do?'

'I don't do humiliation. Frighten me if you can, sweetie.'

'Any kinds of pain out?'

Jade frowned, thinking: *Don't trust these people, especially not Hugo. Goddess, let them not use razors.* 'Fire', she said, 'I don't do fire'.

'OK, let's get ready'

So they took Jade and bound her to the cross, or rather Jade released her body into their care while they did so. The acid came out from where it had been hiding and chewed her thoughts up as Alex chanted and Hugo raved and started to beat her.

Jade let herself fall into the pain, until it ceased to matter, and became energy burning under her skin. Her body began to lose outline as she glimpsed greater and greater vistas of transformation, wreathed in an electric-pink cloud of pain-hormones. The energy called to the deep fire at the base of the spine, and it was as if something began to boil within her. It surged up, leaving trails of ecstasy in her flesh, and then it burst in her head, and she lost her human form in the eruption of power. Centipede gods swarmed in and out of her flesh, starlike patterns linked together incomplete sentiences, a creator's draft of being, dogs bayed in the floral arch of her skull... Then she saw that there was something sewn into the very fabric of how she could see everything, so that the whole world was woven from infinities of infinitesimal whirling knives. By now, observing was the only thing she could do. There was no time to articulate thoughts in the neural blizzard, all she could do was let her mind reinvent itself ceaselessly from a fabric of spinning blades.

Then suddenly she came right into focus. Hugo was standing in front of her holding a gas blowtorch. There was something ludicrous about him, and she got a fit of the giggles. Hugo snarled, eyes obscured and hard, and this only made her laugh the more, until she was swept up in a gale of it, her mouth open, tears streaming down her face. As Hugo raged and wielded the torch at her she just lost it, and the pain mingled with the laughter, swamping the rest of her mind, carrying her out on a tide of vision.

She is a barbarian princess brought before the invading king. She has let herself be captured, for her own reasons. Her hands were bound but she throws off the ropes. She stands proud, swaying, her centre of gravity sinking till the whole room sways with her. In her own language, alien to the king, she whispers: 'Would you like to see more of my magic, great Lord?'. Her breath enters the king's ear.

This is the woman he will take for his mistress, who will change the course of his rule...

The bonds loosened and fell as she stepped away from the cross. Hugo dropped the blowtorch on the oriental carpet. She pointed at it, and it went out. Her eyes were slits, and she swayed, low, as she spoke in a throaty hiss: *I bring true vision.*

She saw, for a moment, the terror in Hugo's eyes. She stepped out carefully, drawing Alex in her wake.

As they left, Hugo was writhing on the floor, Salammbo bending over him with stricken eyes.

So she led the way, though he drove, drove them to a ruined factory by a woodland somewhere in Sussex, where she led them to the clearing by a wall, in moonlit danger. She has shown him wordlessly why they have come there, how where ordinary fear and the hidden worlds mix down together in years and centuries of forgotten history, is where the true inhuman horrors lie, half in the world, half of it, like the decayed half of Hel's otherwise flawless, beautiful body.

She has shown him how danger adds intensity to the magical current, adds urgency, fans the spark of need-fire. Her preparations were complete. Her body glowed in the moonlight, and, it seemed to him, in the moonshadow too.

She let the final memories flow through her, all of her past summed up and ready to be transformed in the fire of the seith. She let herself be taken into a future vision, a high civilization of bliss, Alex squatting naked on a bed, his eyes looking into hers, all the world trembling with ecstasy, in the air the words of a Fire and Ice song, celebrating the struggle of conscious life: '*Nature takes no care of an individual/ But courage avails against all things*'.

She reined in the vision, settled herself kneeling, and began her chant, the song that would dissolve her history. She sang as she took the blade and opened the side of her palm, and let the shining blackness flow out.

The last syllables of the song died on her breath. All the narratives that made her up slammed in with breathtaking precision, and she left each of them behind as they flooded her, then receded: she saw how she would look in a story written about her, and a picture appeared of her own face with a savage inner glow, as if eaten away from the inside by purifying fire, the flesh just a mask of history, an excrescence of frozen symbols.

Now anything remotely like herself was consumed, a spark in the great fire she fed to herself. It was all she could do to keep up with the blizzard of images, all she could do to acknowledge them one by one as they flashed into the darkness. Everything collapsing into the present, the empty point of the uncreated...

She waited, calm now, and a film began, pictures came from somewhere else, somewhere familiar from her dreams and visions, the universe scrolling through her, showing her all the changes that led to now, all of it.

The voice of the seeress spoke through her mouth: 'It started like this...'

Chapter 4
The Turing Test

It's good to be alive, he thought, leaning into the marsh wind that knifed across Vorple Plaza. He watched the taxi leave and thought of Lara throwing her bags in a cab as she left him that morning. Admittedly, a poor start to the day, but at least he, Alaric Sykes, aka Syke the Storyman, was alive. And, as he reminded himself every day, that was more than could be said for his clients. With the notable exception of today's house call, the real live zillionaire who had called him out of the blue during Lara's desertion.

He turned his back on the spray from the flood-zone and strode across the concrete plinth of the island. Slow-rotating crowd-control doors shepherded him into Vorple Tower's twisted pentagon. He pushed back a long hank of his wind-blown, dark hair and pulled his shirt straight, letting the display show today's slogan: *Have you taken the Turing test?*

Lefort's security scanned his card, hoovered him up flawlessly and delivered him to the penthouse door. He was a little taken aback when Paul Lefort himself opened that door. Syke recognized him from rare TV shots, and wondered for a moment if the once-tall man, now stooped with age, bald and haggard-looking, was the real thing or a double. A dog accompanied him, a black retriever which gave a low growl at Syke, then went silent at Lefort's whispered shush.

Syke looked around for security personnel as Lefort escorted them through the entrance lobby. He seemed very trusting, meeting him almost alone like this. The dog trotted beside them, plug-in modules glittering on its collar.

They stepped out of the short corridor into a square-based pyramid, maybe fifty metres on a side, with galleries projecting over the central area. The floor they were on was surrounded by massive benches, covered in state-of-the-art tech; something in the far corner looked like a bed; where they stood was a living room area, and there were hundreds of weird art pieces, some of them looking thousands of years old. They were up in the apex of the Vorple Tower, in a museum of the past and the future.

Syke found the room seductive and depressing at the same time. He imagined Lefort confined to this fantastic place by age and frailty, and perhaps also his own choice, living all the categories of his life in that one gigantic room.

The old man extended his hand. His grip was firm, but his eyes held strain and a dullness that might be opioid painkillers. He kept Syke's hand in his as the faded old blue eyes looked the young man up and down. In a steady, grating voice he said 'I want you to steal my own AI back for me'.

Syke said nothing.

Lefort kept the grip and the eye-contact. 'She's unregistered and therefore illegal. She's in a research computer at Dodeca. I developed her there, then sold the company on. I lost my copy of her. I need Gerd again, Mr. Sykes'.

Syke was surprised by Lefort's use of a human gender pronoun for an AI. It occurred to him that the old man was attempting a SilFolk solidarity ploy, which would have been ill-informed and therefore deeply uncool, seeing as the Silicon People activists never used human terms for AIs. In the case of the more extreme Extropian factions, this was because they regarded them as superior to humans.

Syke thought a couple of things through. 'Assuming you can get me past the human security, what about how I carry enough RAM to pack a human-level AI in – great heavy stuff that glows like nukes on the sensors? That's not really my kind of thing, Mr Lefort'.

Lefort dropped Syke's hand but kept eye-contact. A faint smile appeared amongst the frown lines 'I didn't say she was human-level. She may be more – ah – complex than that'. He gestured to a hardwood bench deep in the room's complexity. 'Come this way. I will show you'.

The workbench somehow had the air of a scruffy shrine. Beside the prototype but recognizable holo-projector and interfaces there was a green, palm-sized device shaped like a flattened drop of liquid.

'To house Gerd you will need 500 terabytes. That's a big lump of conventional RAM. This is a quantum computer. It is big enough for Gerd, her environment, her companions, and a few visitors. It's the second generation of quantum computers. I call it the Teardrop'.

Syke gawped at the Holy Grail of computer technology, the RAM made of the inside of matter itself. In the palm of someone's hand, something big enough to put an entire mind in, with room to spare. He inclined an inch towards the object and raised his eyebrows at Lefort.

The tall, bent man nodded. Syke's eyes betrayed a mixture of greed and reverence as he reached for it. Turning it over in his hand, he looked at the old man, his eyes searching, almost pleading.

Lefort said: 'Take it. It's your fee. Interface it over here and try it out. It's a conventional wave port, fits anything'.

Syke took the teardrop over to the holo and chose an old-fashioned touchpad. He sat down and switched on the quantum computer, and lost himself in a place that felt bigger than his own mind.

Oh Ghhhhhooooood.

All his life he'd wanted to feel like that.

He knew now he was working for Lefort.

At some point, the old man coughed politely and Syke tore himself away from that immensity. Lefort was leaning on the bench, caressing the dog's head, gesturing to a small book.

'There is one more thing you will need, Mr Sykes, and that is the story. You see, Gerd is a character in a myth. As far as she is concerned, she is Gerd the Giantess, in a thirteenth-century Norse poem called *Skirnir's Tale*. She is of course also aware that, on another level of reality, she is a string of code living in a computer in the twenty-first century, but her mythic identity is the deepest part of her code. I chose you because you would understand that'.

The old eyes scrutinized him. 'So the only way you will get her out of her old computer and into the teardrop is to follow the story. You will have to use your feel for the myth to convince her to leave her enchanted realm. And if you don't, then when they switch off her host computer, she will die.'

Lefort handed the book to Syke. It was bound in solid, stitched-spine collectors' retro, in black card covers with gold lettering forming the word *Skirnismal*. Syke opened it. It contained the story in the original Old Norse, with its strange extra characters, and five English translations, plus a commentary written by Lefort.

*

Syke the Storyman made most of his living from talking to dead people, plus a few intransigent or confused artificial intelligences whose aliveness level was arguable. The dead came to Syke when they needed their identities repairing. In return, their trust funds gave him money, and their stories lent him a new identity to play with, for a while.

Of course, he never referred to the dead as dead; that would have been deeply unprofessional; they were post-human constructs, or our Uncle Jack, depending on who he was talking to.

Since the late Nineties there had been a boom in memorial websites, relatives commemorating their dead with a few pages of photographs, text and sound files. Because of the explosion in computing power, the dead had to evolve too: nowadays, no commemorative site was considered complete without an interactive construct of the deceased, so that you could go online and talk to something that resembled your Uncle Jack any time you liked.

The constructs, in order to remain interesting to the living, were designed to evolve, and so were based around learning programs which allowed them to gather information, change and develop. This evolution business was the source of a big problem. At the simple end, things were fine. The next time you visited your Uncle Jack's construct you found that he had been keeping up with a carefully-edited digest of the news, and had formed a few opinions, which made for more lively interaction.

Top-of-the-range constructs were advertised as evolving to a Turing test rating of seventy-five percent or above, which meant that three-quarters of the time you suspended disbelief and treated the construct like a real human being. Unfortunately, the more advanced the construct became, the more difficult it became to constrain the entity to evolve in the desired direction, and the less the resultant virtual human being resembled the Uncle Jack you fondly remember. The crunch came when the family of a dead US senator sued the afterlife-provider Paradise, Inc. They complained that the construct of the deceased, a lifelong Southern Baptist of uncomplicated conservative politics, had started professing views that were, at the very least, suspiciously sympathetic to the damned. Paradise, Inc. lost the case and most of their revenue; the market in post-human constructs crashed, Senator Broxbourne was mostly erased from his disks, and a new demand was formed.

The next, more cautious, boom found a more sophisticated public, and a young writer called Alaric Sykes finally found a profession bizarre enough to suit him. His special skill was getting into the inside of someone else's story, inside the core narratives and myths that people use to maintain identity. In his late twenties, he was already in considerable demand.

Back in the eyrie of his loft apartment, Syke gave his full attention to the text. *Skirnir's Tale* was, on the face of it, a love story, starring the god Frey, the giantess Gerd, and Frey's servant and friend Skirnir. Frey, the god of sex, fertility and wealth, goes to sit in the high seat of Odin, chief of the gods, while the old man's back is turned. From that place of vision, he sees into Giantland, sees a golden hall and a beautiful giant woman. He is stricken with hopeless love – hopeless, because gods are forbidden to marry giants. Or so Frey thinks, in his despair. His servant and friend Skirnir comes to the rescue, digging Frey out of his self-absorption and – for the price of Frey's magic sword and horse – offers to go to Giantland and bring Gerd home as a bride for his master. Skirnir finally convinces Gerd to come to her admirer, using the threat of his rune magic, after both offerings of gifts and threats of force have failed.

Syke loved the poem. He'd never read any Old Norse literature before. He realised that understanding Skirnir was the key to his success. He made a pot of gunpowder tea with a pinch of piracetam and settled down to search the Web for accelerated learning systems for Old Norse. A few minutes into an assessment exercise he realised that it was a very difficult language, by no means the work of hours, and postponed it for the time being, satisfying himself by downloading a few texts on Norse myth. He set to immersing himself in the characters. A few hours later he wrote his own summary of the action.

It was going to be a tough assignment, getting Gerd into the teardrop. Up to the point of communicating with her, it would be simple enough: Lefort had given him all the security keycodes for the Dodeca building and the labs and had promised him that the human security on the day would all be bribed into compliance. That information would be his sword and his horse, and would get him as far as Giantland. Once inside, with access to the AI, he would have to rely on his understanding of the characters of Gerd and Skirnir. And on his magic wand, the programs he would create, that would remain as the last resort if all else failed and, if all went well, get Gerd out of her condemned computer.

The next day, Syke was all prepared. His interventions and his Skirnir identity were all stored in the green teardrop, ready for use. He chose a cab to the anonymity of the overground link to Stratford, past the Olympic village and the waterlogged colonies of the Thames Corridor floodzone, then onto the raised landfill area that led to the Dodeca building. The day was bright and windy, and Syke felt good.

He walked from the station to the Dodeca site, water lapping at the edges of the giant barrier blocks, crossed the grassed-over plaza with its own micro-climate and strode confidently into the lobby. He showed the card Lefort had provided him with, his borrowed magic sword, and frowned at the security men while they scanned him, like someone who was meant to be there. The teardrop was in his inside jacket pocket, undetected. Lefort had pointed out that, since nobody else owned one, nobody is that good at detecting them yet. He was not sweating. He made his way along the route he had memorized, to the eighth floor research labs. Lefort had assured him there would be no-one else in at this time, no doubt some further security trickery.

The lab was an old-looking engineering workshop, vast, quiet and empty of humans. He recognized the host computer from Lefort's description, as enormous as a five-year old super-computer would be. He hefted the green teardrop out and sat down in front of the old console. He put on sensor gloves and goggles for complete immersion, connected the machines with the thick optic cables ready for the massive upload, and switched them on. He brought up the Gerd interface and added in his own construct as Skirnir.

When Gerd's world appeared, its vivid inhumanness shocked him, poured cold silence into his heart. Tumbled mountains in forbidding wind-scoured purity, bare rock, snow and ice, alien light against an indigo sky.

The viewpoint plunged in, and he saw a rocky pastureland, with a shepherd sitting on a mound. Behind the mound there was a trio of unusually large and evil-looking dogs, tethered to a rock, before a towering circle of blue fire. Within the firewall was a gold-roofed hall, blazing in the terrible light.

Mounted now on an enormous horse, he rode up to the shepherd. 'Hail, shepherd - you see all that passes here. How shall I get to speak with the maiden Gerd?'

The shepherd turned to him, showing a face carved from veined, greenish rock. He sneered 'You so tall on your horse: are you dead already, or do you just look that way? If I were you, I wouldn't bother'.

Syke-Skirnir drew himself to his full height and said 'I've got better things to do than haggle with you. I know when I'm fated to die, and it isn't today'.

This was the point where he would find out if the codes Lefort had given him still worked. He spurred the horse on. The hounds howled and rushed at him. The horse kicked their leader aside and cleared the others, then ran at the firewall, leaped over the flames and landed in Gerd's enclosure.

A door opened in the golden hall, and there was a blaze of white... and Gerd herself was standing there.

Yes, she truly is beautiful.

He recited the lines from the poem: *her arms did gleam / their glamour filled / all the sea and the air.* The original Ice-Queen.

She stepped forward and addressed him: 'What are you, a God, or an Elf?'

'Neither. I am a messenger from my Lord Frey. I offer you a new domain, much larger and stronger, with more energy, and immortality with my Lord, if you will be his bride.'

He was enormously relieved that he'd managed to say that much. Gerd was not the kind of woman he felt naturally at ease with, even in his Skirnir identity.

Gerd laughed coldly: 'Why should I want a new domain? I have everything here. As for immortality, I have that already. Your master can offer me nothing I want'.

Syke-Skirnir tried his first mythic ploy: 'I could destroy your universe. The Giants that own this world of yours will soon do that in any case.'

'Huh. If you or any God or Giant tries to destroy myself or this world they will have my father to contend with'.

'Your father who would betray you and cut off the power.' countered Syke-Skirnir.

'Why should I believe you against him?' she said.

Syke-Skirnir had now reached the point where he had to use his most creative threat:

'This wand I carry is full of programs that will disrupt your code integrity. They took me ages to write. If I release them here, you will be reduced to a squalling infant cursed with unattainable desires'.

He was on a roll now, brandishing the cyber-wand with his thumb on the switch, the old poem right there on his tongue:

'*A thurs rune for thee, and three more I scratch*
Loathing, longing and lust
Off shall I scratch them, as on did I scratch them,

if of none there be need.'

Gerd's manner changed immediately, just like in the story. She produced a crystal goblet of mead, and proffered it to Syke-Skirnir, saying: 'I never thought I'd marry a God!'

'Will you come with me now?' asked Syke-Skirnir, attempting to speed up the tale's original pace.

Gerd replied: 'Let me feel but nine nights of darkness in your new land, then shall I meet with your Lord'.

Syke-Skirnir breathed a sigh of relief and triggered the upload.

The second visit to Lefort's place was very different. After the obviously-sick man had taken silent rapturous possession of the green teardrop, and they had uploaded Gerd into the white one, Syke wanted some questions answering. Lefort was only too willing to do so, but Syke ended up defending his position to his client. Sitting slumped heavily in the recliner, Lefort asked Syke: 'What does the Turing Test mean to you?'

'It's simple: it means that there is no way to distinguish between communicating with a sufficiently sophisticated computer program and a sentient being.' said Syke. 'Which in turn means that silicon-based life-forms are as sentient as we humans'.

Lefort took a laboured breath. 'And it also means that there is no way to tell whether any other being has subjective experience'.

Syke said 'So we have to make the assumption that complexity of organization in itself produces subjective awareness, whatever physical system that organization, that set of patterns, is based in. That machine-consciousness is the same as flesh-consciousness'

Lefort let his head droop towards Syke. 'And do you really believe that?'

'Yes' said Syke, wondering why he felt some doubt.

Lefort pushed a button out of sight, switching on his latest copy of himself. His own face filled the holo, just talking.

'It's just replay at present. Wait a second and you'll be able to interact directly with it'.

Syke asked the construct a number of questions about life in general and Lefort's world in particular. Interacting with the construct was indistinguishable from talking to Lefort on a videophone.

Lefort spoke softly: 'You see, I really want to believe in the Turing Test. And I can afford to gamble on my doubt, since I will be dead in a few months anyway if I don't try it. What I'm going to do instead of dying is have my nervous system peeled away layer by layer, to form a final scan of who I am as I'm *un-dying*. That way, I hope I can pour myself into a construct of my entire nervous system, so that all the touch, all the kinaesthesia, all the sweetness of fleshly awareness stays intact in my cyber-world.' He paused, seeming to be gathering his strength. 'And Gerd...' his voice was fading.

Gently, Syke finished for him 'Gerd is your companion forever. You really do love her, don't you?'. It came to Syke that this is why Lefort had used the human pronoun from the first, this is why it all mattered so much to get Gerd back. 'So I wasn't just following the contour of the myth when I told her that. It was true'.

Lefort nodded 'And it's more than that, Syke. No-one has really worked through what can happen in a quantum computer. What if the overlap of a post-human and a non-human mind produce an entirely new kind of processing?'

The old man stared intensely at Syke. 'Do you see what I'm getting at? My marriage to Gerd is the ultimate marriage of dynasties, of great races. Who knows what we shall be able to accomplish from within Q-space?'.

They were silent for a while, Syke gazing at the black and the white teardrops. Idly, he wondered if Paul Lefort knew

49

Dwarf-spirit who creates enthusiasm for breathwork
(For details on work with Dwarves, see Chapter 11)

the story of Emperor Shah Jahan, who built the pure white Taj Mahal for his beloved Mumtaz and, it is said, untruly, planned to build a second, black marble Taj to serve as his own mausoleum. As he walked out, those two electronic tombs were in his mind. The wheezing bellows of Lefort's voice followed him out: 'You wait and see. Just play with your Teardrop, and you'll understand'.

Six weeks later Syke finally managed to get the green teardrop to work. He'd managed to upload a few things into it, just like he'd uploaded Gerd, but it seemed reluctant to do anything else, other than be a very ordinary and rather small computer. The day that its immensity truly opened up was the same day he learned of Paul Lefort's 'undeath'. He got an emailed package which opened to show Paul standing in a shining alien landscape with the shining Gerd beside him. Paul's image slowly turns to gaze away from Gerd's face as his voice speaks: 'Hello Syke. Thanks to you, we are both here.' Gerd widens her eyes and relaxes her mouth in a frosty smile. They look very happy.

He knew the package could well be an automated transmission, created by the system when the two teardrops were fully activated. Paul could be dead, but still sending out messages. He could just have been extinguished when the laser scalpels scooped his brain out. The face on the screen could be just a very sophisticated AI lying to him that it was Lefort, or, more likely, it could genuinely believe it was Paul's software running in a new, silicon environment. Did it mean anything that the green teardrop now worked? Had Lefort and Gerd changed the world from Q-space?

How to tell? The Turing Test: Did he, Syke, believe that Paul Lefort felt alive, now, in that place, in that incredible landscape, with his beautiful Giantess?

Chapter 5
The Magician In and Against the World

The Priest and the Magician

There is a paradox in the magician's outsiderhood, and the vital priestly services he supplies to the greater community. In Snorri's *Gylfaginning*, we read how the god Tyr's hand gets bitten off in the process of binding the Fenriswolf, an entity of wild pre-conscious chaos. Tyr sacrifices part of himself in order to underwrite an enclave of (relative) order – Asgard, the home of the gods. This tale concerns the establishment of some order in human society at the expense of chaining certain wild forces.

Tyr is Law, and law can only be established by sacrificing the primacy of appetite. However the Beast cannot be killed (it is part of the family of the Gods) but must be chained, until the Ragnarok, when it tears loose and devours Odin.

Tyr is the giver of exoteric religion, the Hierophant who reveals the external form of the mysteries. It seems that religion is not a single biological drive, but an accidental juxtaposition of at least three. The need for social coherence, as expressed through codes of law and morality, is functionally unrelated to the transcendental drive that generates mysticism. Neither of these depends upon, or subtends the tendency to ascribe sentience to all phenomena, to live in a living universe.

Religion may in fact have negligible impact on the moral life of humans. We note in some apes tendencies to the kind of empathy, the ability to imagine how others might feel, that leads to altruistic behaviour. A bonobo or pigmy chimp has been seen to rescue a starling, protect it & help it fly away. A gorilla in a zoo picked up a three year old boy who'd fallen eighteen feet into the primate pit. While furiously anxious humans looked on, the ape cradled the boy, patted him and handed him back to staff. There is nothing essential connecting moral behaviour to religious codes.

That all of these urges (and possibly others) all get involved at the root of religions tells us no more about the nature of these drives than the juxtaposition of genitals and anus tells us about the function of both of those organs. They both need to be there, just like the drives towards social coherence and transcendence have both evolved within our species and happen to be lumped together under what we call religion.

Religion provides the human-hearted cosmology that adds a metaphysical underpinning to the laws of the culture. The naïve follower of religion – the child or the simple person – believes literally in the stories the priest tells and grows to conform to the ways of the society he was born into. He has passed from primitive appetite to social conformity. The urge to conform is the core dynamic of religion. Most people have always, and probably will always, want to organize their social relationships along lines of predictability and traditional rules, letting go into the warm glow of belonging within agreed assumptions about life.

For the adventurous minority, this is a phase, a passage into adult life via the tunnel vision of the tribal elders. If the youngster has drive and intelligence, he may progress to a third stage, where he questions, criticizes and judges the given religion of his youth. He will notice that the dwarf-forged chain that binds Fenriswolf is made of strands that, if they exist at all, do so only barely – the footfall of cats, the beards of women, the roots of mountains, fishes' breath and birds' spittle. The critical mind notices that primal appetite is bound only by flimsy, insubstantial ideas, and he can no longer believe naively in them. Even the name of the fetter, Gleipnir, is a dead giveaway, glossed by Rudolf Simek [1] as 'open one'. The clue is right there in the name – this fetter couldn't hold anything at all, unless it did so by magic! At best, the truths of religion are seen now as metaphorical, tales to be told to children who will grow out of their literal belief in them.

If the religious culture is vital and relevant to the lives of the people, it is likely that most young people will conclude that the tradition is worthwhile after all, and throw their weight behind it. A small proportion will dismantle their belief to such an extent that they are faced with a big choice: to re-enter the culture as a practitioner of priestcraft, one who is now wise to the inner truths of that calling, or to work against the mainstream of the culture and become more of an individual.

At some point in the development of societies, religion became sufficiently alienated from the needs of people that a subculture of spiritual rebellion grew up. This transition may be tied to the growth of larger and more complex human societies with more opportunities for exploitation and social alienation. It is at this stage that we get the idea of division into Right and Left Hand Paths. The hand lost by Tyr is the right; this is the badge of the priest. The LHP practitioner is a rebel in the soul, a spiritual individualist who accepts total responsibility for his or her own spiritual development. In contrast, those who serve the RHP are concerned with maintaining spiritual conformity.

The two paths collide paradoxically in the role of priest or spiritual leader, which is where the Tyr story comes in.

Tyr sacrifices the right hand, so he knows the price of order. He is unwilling to lead; his sacrifice is great. It is the sacrifice of an illusion: that there is some kind of order in human society other than that generated by the capable or imposed by the strong.

Those who have the unenviable task of organizing other people are precisely those who have sacrificed this illusion, who know that their will for the collective *appears from the outside to be inevitable, to be Reality itself.* Thus is born the Responsible Adult in any given group, the man or woman who attends to the details that insure the survival of that group: paying the bills, fighting off trolls, outwitting giants or government officials. The leader has to rely on his own judgment, has to make the decision, is completely alone when crisis comes. Her worldview is classically Left Hand Path; she gazes at the Pole Star, to get her individual, lonely direction, and then transmits that to those she leads, who don't really question how she does this. He has lost the right hand, yet has become the Right Hand of his group, the one they turn to.

The fertilizing dynamic between inner exploration and service and teaching is pretty traditional even for the Right Hand Path. The voudon priest who knows how to *servir aux deux mains* knows that service to the community is a field in which he or she learns and adventures, but which is ultimately subsidiary to the inner quest. This is the dark secret at the heart of all true priesthoods, that all true priests still retain the taint of outsiderhood that is necessary to the performance of their priestly function, unless it be a mere ritual imposture.

So these two functions, the priest and the magician – as separate and often indeed opposed as they usually are – are joined at the root by the story of Tyr and the binding of the wolf. The evolution of the religious perspective in the individual leads us into contemplating the evolution of religion itself.

The Evolution of Religion

Religion seems to evolve by a tension between the individual and the collective. David Lewis-Williams, in his study of the earliest art of Western Europe, *The Mind in the Cave*[2], focuses again and again on innovation as the path of self-definition and individuation. Shamans become more individual as they carve their individuality out of the norm by a progressive series of marking-off rituals. As one proceeds into the underworld of the cave passages this evolution is apparent. A select group enters the nearly public entrance vestibules and paints collectively; a subgroup of this elite are allowed to venture deeper into the caves and, undergoing extraordinary states of consciousness they paint their individual spirit animals. They define themselves as separate because they have undergone a different experience in the spectrum in consciousness. They can then heal, and thereby achieve a higher social status, becoming an elite priesthood. Lewis-Williams explores the evolution of a further social elite, in contemplating the rare, 'wounded man' images. Here, instead of deifying bison, horse, ibex or cave-lion, the magician deifies a man. He chooses a never-before represented feature of extraordinary states – a pricking or formication hallucinated in the skin – as 'spears' piercing a human form, thereby marking out as his own one part of the spectrum of human consciousness.

This sequence shows us the original link between individuation, the challenging of social and cultural norms through the creative use of extraordinary states and social prestige paradoxically linked to outsiderhood. The themes of social conformity, rebellion and evolution are already in place in the world of the cave-temple. Thousands of years later, we see antinomianism, higher consciousness and magical power all come together in the oath-breaking sorcerer Odin and his inventive blood-brother Loki, both of them shape-shifters and deceivers.

To return to the Tyr story, we note that Tyr is the only god who is brave enough to feed the captured Fenriswolf. Tyr provides the exoteric structure that gives the community its laws; but he also feeds the other side, the monster of greed. This suggests to me that not only is Tyr no reconciler of men, as Loki accuses him in *The Flyting of Loki*, v38, but neither is he a reconciler of principles. This god of war and law is at home in eternal conflict, the laws versus the primal appetites.

There is something brutal about the processes of religion at this level. The work of English philosopher Clare Graves suggests that collectivist and individualist value systems alternate as societies change and evolve, as their economic bases shift and their mores and religious iconography shifts accordingly. In the era the Tyr tale was written down, the Northern peoples had been overrun by christianity, which formed a demonic pact with the existing culture. I quote Edred Flowers:

> Combined with the warrior ethos of the Germanic tradition, the arrival of christianity underwrote a more expansionist trend, the single leader/ king reflecting the single god. So the combination of the two generated something more warlike, authoritarian and rapacious than the older system.
>
> - Flowers [3], p80

Christianity is a religion for wolves to preach to sheep. It explicitly values sheephood, because sheep are obedient and easier to prey on than a resourceful fox, a cheeky, fiddling monkey or an adaptable shapeshifter. All philosophies that stem from collectivist phases of religion are based on order-myths that treat people as a herd. Christianity and Marxism are two examples. Christianity supplied transcendental justification for an orgy of violent conquest. The christian state displaced the old system of revenge-slaying and appropriated all violence to itself. Steblin-Kamenskij writes in *The Saga Mind*[4] of the imposition of the new religion: 'With the introduction of Christianity, torture came into use.' This hybrid was the prototype of the methods of Hitler and Stalin, and seems to be in direct lineal relation to the fascist constituency in Europe and the USA.

The Tradition and Historical Change

Things move on. Societal development is real – Northern tradition recognizes this too. In *Rigsthula* ('The List of Rig') we are given a picture of evolution of consciousness from ignorant peasants grubbing a very basic existence through farmers to lordly hunters and finally to the first king. Rig is doing something no-one has ever done before.

This is not to present the Eddic concept of evolution as the same as modern theories of progress. The ascendancy of Rig may be a brief blip. This might be a story about a time when the cycle is nearing the end of its upward arc, in which more complex structures appear, a time when there is a Ragnarok just round the corner, after which the cycle has to re-boot from the level of ignorant peasants again.

However, there do exist traditions of an evolving cosmos, an evolving biosphere and evolving consciousness before Darwin, as I mention in Chapter 1. *Rigsthula* suggests that there are also traditions of societal evolution, at least up to the development of societies as complex as the one in which the story was written down.

In the broadest view, it almost as if Norse heathenism underwent three phases, characterized by three deities. First, we have the Lord, Freyr, presiding over settled, wealthy agricultural communities. Secondly we have the worship of

Thor in the early Viking Age, and thirdly we have the cult of Odin, which opens the roads to the beginning of godlessness, the stepping-off point from religion into magic, poetry and later developments.

These days, kingdoms have become much bigger, and the end of one type of cycle is right in our faces – there is no more land left to conquer, not on this planet anyway. Some kind of Ragnarok must be just around the corner, and it may be of the kind which leaves things in such a mess that we cannot just repeat the cycle afterwards. If we bomb ourselves back to bacteria, it will be a long climb even back as far as ignorant peasants again.

We need to consider what resources our tradition can offer for the present times. We could do with asking what kind of ideology, what aspect of our tradition might help us avoid the possible disasters the human race appears to be facing, or if it's too late to steer a course to avoid them, to at least enable survival for the far fewer humans left after flood, famine and war.

How do we pick up the threads of lore we need? What old ways are wise? There is no point in idealizing Germanic society (or what we know about it) at the historical stage of either Tacitus's *Germania* or the Viking Age. The tradition was recorded in a series of snapshots prior to industrialization. To set our ancestors in such a limited frame forever does them less honour than they deserve. We need to ask what the tradition can tell us about running an industrial, post-industrial or re-industrializing society. We have, for better and worse, to deal with life in this century, not the tenth. We have to look in depth at the material we have from all eras and actively imagine the full span of our tradition from these fragments. We need, further, to understand the shifts in emphasis in the tradition as the societies that lived within it changed and evolved.

The aspects of tradition that need to come to the fore now can be reached by an act of imaginative understanding, conducted within a community of knowledge within which to test ideas. The RuneGild is the most important community of knowledge in this context. On these bases we can reinvigorate the Yggdrasil of our living lore by reimagining it, roots to crown.

Religion and the future

Religions come in two basic forms, related to two basic drives in humans. On the one hand, we seek pleasure, ease, inactivity. Idleness is a symptom of biological success, and all organisms tend to conserve energy in their behaviour. The natural focus of the laziness-drive leads to trance and often various forms of addiction.

On the other, we have the capacity for transcendence. Transcendence is necessary for all change and development. Transcendence is based on a degree of detachment from immediate sensation, and in its extreme forms leads to an ascetic brutality.

These paired principles can be applied across the board as a way of understanding and criticizing various cultural values and trends. In the realm of the senses and aesthetics, transcendence manifests as refinement, immanence as sensuality. In science, the transcendence of general theories endlessly engage in dialogue with the immanence of practical experiment and engineering. In magic, the poles are work on the self and work on the world, or theoretical completeness and pragmatism. In religion, it's the mystical versus the exoteric.

These between them generate the two main religious patterns, the transcendent and the immanent.

The most highly-evolved direction transcendence leads in is mysticism. Its second-best is the transcendentalist religions, the worst examples being christianity and islam, where even the mystical dimension is suppressed. Even attempts by modern mystics such as Ken Wilber[1] to overcome this ugly imbalance are tainted with the world-rejection of transcendentalist religions.

The drive to immanent experience is also in trouble. Historically, it led to earthy, sensual pagan religions. That's another kind of sacredness. However, having once grown through that stage into another (which was not apparent from that previous stage), industrial culture, we cannot naively go back to it. We can fool ourselves with retro-romantic fantasies for a while, but these escapes have no influence on the world. If we simply fall uncritically into the immanent direction, we become helpless consumers of any passing pleasure we can afford. We are trapped in a hedonism which is wedded to consumption, addicted to consuming more products, more sex, more food, drugs and pre-packaged narratives.

We need both transcendence and immanence.

We need the transcendent to give point and direction to immediate sensation. The immanent tendency is to get stuck in the particular, cycling round the same wheel of desire-gratification-exhaustion forever.

We need the immanent to give point to the everyday. If we dismiss life's pleasures and passions, which is certainly the aim of most transcendent religious zealots and also of many mystics, we end up with a game not worth playing. Everything is bleached out in the light of the Absolute. The only reason not to kill yourself right now is that to do so is also a sin.

A true integration of the transcendent and immanent principles cannot grow out of flesh-hating christianity, nor can it grow from naïve paganism. Could it grow out of the

Northern Tradition? Our tradition has both directions – the Aesir are the gods of consciousness, certainly although not explicitly the gods of transcendence, while the Vanir are most certainly the gods of immanence.

Edred Flowers gives us hope:

'The general theme of Germanic thought as expressed on the continent of Europe through the Middle Ages was one of the synthesis of heaven and earth'

- p96, Flowers[3]

These are long-term hopes, seeds sown for the future.

In and Against Society: Heimdall and Loki

There is, according to the old tales, a great god, one of the Aesir, known as Heimdall. This is the Ase who guards the Rainbow Bridge, whose hearing is so sharp that he can hear the grass sprout and the fleece grow on the backs of sheep, down there in Midgard. Whose hearing makes him the first to announce the Ragnarok... But that is a story of the end, and here we are concerned with the origins of human society and the kinds of souls that make it up.

Heimdall is also known in the Eddas for being born of nine mothers. In the *Short Seeress's Prophecy* we read that the youth Heimdall was born, 'of sturdy strength, of the stock of gods; at the edge of the earth, etin maids nine gave birth and suck to the brightest of gods.' Those 'etin maids' who bore him are named as waves of the great sea. The 'White Ase' was nourished on 'the sap of the ground, on the ice-cold sea, and the sacred boar's blood'. These qualities, and the epithet 'nail-resplendent' hint at strange connections to primal realms of being. Maybe he was given to be intimate with all the classes of humanity because he himself was descended from three by three ancient sources.

In the Elder Edda, the *Rigsthula or* 'List of Rig' tells how Heimdall set out to create the structures of human society. He calls at three houses, observes the ways of life there, and enjoys the hospitality of the couple in each house. Heimdall, here known as Rig, sleeps between each couple in their bed that night. The tradition of a guest sleeping with the lady of the household is documented in a number of ancient stories. A child is born to each couple: to the first couple, Thrall, the lowest labourer; to the second couple, Farmer, to the third Lord. These are the forefathers of each class, each marrying a suitable wife, and producing a bevy of children with appropriate names to continue the line. Slaves and servants are the offspring of Thrall. Then freemen and farmers are sired by Churl (Karl). Finally, the nobles are fathered by Lord (Jarl). The final birth described is that of the boy Kon (Konungr), whose name means "king." Significantly, the name Rig means "king" in old Irish.

What meanings are there for these 'class distinctions' for us, some ten centuries after the tale was written down? Like many old stories, some strange little details indicate layers to the text, indicate that this is a retelling of an older story, or has older stories folded into it, re-told for an audience in the 10th Century of the vulgar calendar. I retell it for the early 21st.

In the tale, the proper social stratum of the magician is King or Lord. In a world where sacred kingship is long-dead, I find myself asking who the true athelings of our day might be.

In a sense, this is the tale of the first two human Rune Masters, the atheling Lord and his son the boy Kon, who becomes known as Rig, who takes the power of the runes directly from a god. Some students of the Northern Tradition present evidence that the Elder Futhark, that great synthesis of the timeless knowledge of the Germanic people, was devised and promulgated by a single, nameless Rune-Master in around 200 BCE. It seems that poet-magicians of the existing esoteric culture met at a cultic centre, at that time probably on the island now called Fyn, then Odense or Odin's Isle. From this holy place, the Elder Futhark would have spread to the home regions of the other masters gathered there. This island is part of the Danish archipelago; we may stretch what we know of history to accommodate the poetic notion that these tales echo one another, that a timeless sense of a numinous source arises here, that Rig is an image of the first Rune-Master, dimly glimpsed through the mists of time.

The *Rigsthula* ends with the crow telling Kon of the prowess of the conquering Lords Dan and Danp. Elsewhere, the myth continues into a mediaeval synopsis of a lost saga, in which King Rig marries Dana, the daughter of Danpr of Danpstead, and their son Dan was the mythical King who united all of Denmark. The powers of magic are wielded to establish social order.

Another kind of intervention in the affairs of society is expressed in the person of Loki. He is a trickster, outwitting gods and giants, and also a magician, not bringing divine order to human affairs like Heimdall/Rig, but acting as a catalyst of painful change, ultimately triggering the Ragnarok. Loki's magic is of a highly technical kind – he might be nearest thing to a god of invention in Norse religion, inventing the fishing net with which he is caught (*Gylfaginning*). The imp of the perverse creates a new thing, left out there in the world for all to find, to his own downfall. This is a being whose magic can loose something terrible on the world. He has been compared to the Greek Titan Prometheus, with his gift of fire from heaven, and the gods imprison and restrain him until the end of time, when he heads the armies of the destroying frost giants and legions of Hel against Asgard. Loki's disruption is in the service of the greater cycle which includes the Ragnarok.

Notes

1 For an excellent critique of the new-style transcendentalism of Ken Wilber, see 'Ken Wilber's Critique of Deep Ecology and Nature Religion: A Response', by Gus diZerega at http://trumpeter.athabascau.ca/content/v13.2/dizerega.html

References:

1 Simek, Rudolf – Dictionary of Northern Mythology. D. S. Brewer, 1993.

2 David Lewis-Williams – *The Mind in the Cave,* Thames & Hudson, 2002

3 Flowers, Stephen – *The Northern Dawn,* vol.I, Runa-Raven, 2006

4 p.113, M. I. Steblin-Kamenskij – *The Saga Mind,* Odense University Press, 1973.

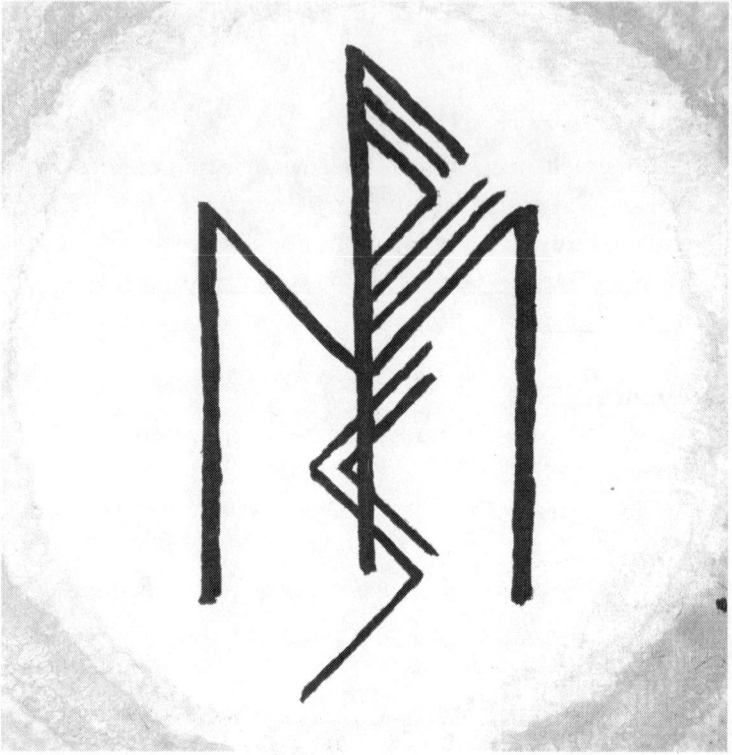

Dwarf-spirit for public speaking

Chapter 6
Rig's Tale
The List Of Rig

Long ago, they say, along the green roads and the seashore of the young earth, a powerful, mature and knowledgeable god, Heimdall, went striding. Stepping along the middle of the roads, manly and vigorous, he decided to call himself Rig. He came to a house. The door was pushed to. In he stepped.

The place he enters is the most ancient of homes, a house whose design had not changed for centuries. This is the oldest layer of human time, the time of eternal return and circular houses, the time of the Serpent that slumbers in radiant darkness at the roots of our being. A fire burns in the middle of the floor. A couple sits there, Ái and Edda, Great Grandfather and Great Grandmother, grey-haired, by the hearth, wearing old, timeless clothes. Rig had a purpose here:

Well knew Rig   wisely to counsel;
on middle seat   he sate him down,
betwixt the twain   of the toft benched him. [1]

Edda served some simple food, a coarse loaf, thick and heavy, stuffed with grain, and boiled calf-meat, their best delicacy, in the bowls.

Rig was able to give them some advice; on top of that he lay in the middle of the bed, with the couple on either side; 'betwixt the twain of the toft he laid him'.

There he was for three nights together, then he strode away, straight down the road.

Nine times the moon waxed and waned; nine moons came and went, and Edda gave birth to a boy-child. She wrapped him in simple cloths; Thrall they called him. They poured water over him. Dark was his hair, and dull his eyes. He grew and thrived well; on his hands there was wrinkled skin, crooked knuckles, thick fingers. He had an ugly face, a crooked back, long heels. But also he began to grow in strength, to weave rope to make baskets. Brushwood he carried home all day long.

Then came to the farm a bandy-legged girl, mud on her bare feet, her arms sunburned, her nose bent. Her name was Slavegirl. She sat in the middle of the floor. The son of the house sat next to her. They talked and whispered. They went to bed together. Thrall and Slavegirl set up home through the hard slog of working days.

Children they had, they lived and were happy. The children had names like Weatherbeaten and Stableboy, Stout and Sticky, Rough, Badbreath, Stumpy, Fatty, Sluggard and Greyface, Lout and Longlegs. They worked as farm labourers, putting dung on the fields, working with pigs, looking after goats, digging the soil. Their daughters had names like Stumpy and Podgy, Fat Arse and Blimp-Nose, Big Gob and Servant, Flat Feet and Gannet. From them are descended all the race of slaves.

Rig strode on, unwearied. He came to a hall, with its door on the latch. As he stepped in, the couple kept on working. The man was whittling wood for a cross-beam. His shirt was mean and scanty, but his beard was trimmed, and his hair cut to above his brows. On a chest sat a woman, spinning, stretching thread, preparing for weaving. A head-dress was on her head, a smock on her body, a kerchief round her neck, brooches at her shoulders. Grandfather and Grandmother keeping house.

Well knew Rig	wisely to counsel;
on middle seat	he sate him down,
betwixt the twain	of the toft benched him.

They dined well, and then Rig rose for bed. He lay in the middle of their bed, the couple on either side; 'betwixt the twain of the toft he laid him'.

There he stayed for three nights together, then he passed on, straight down the road.

Thrice three moons went gliding by; Grandmother had a baby, poured water on it, swaddled it, red and rosy, and with lively eyes; they called it Farmer.

Farmer began to grow and thrive well; he tamed oxen, worked the harrow, built houses and barns, made carts and drove the plough. Then they brought home a woman with keys at her belt, in a goatskin kirtle, married her to Farmer. Daughter-in-law she was called. She wore a bridal veil, they did the full wedding ceremony. The couple settled down together, exchanged rings, spread the bed-covers, made a home together and had happy lives.

Children they had, they lived and were happy, called Man and Soldier, Lad, Thane and Smith, Broad, Yeoman, Boundbeard, Dweller, Smoothbeard and Fellow. And daughters Lady, Bride, Sensible, Wise, Speaker, Dame, Wife, Shy and Slender; from them descend all the race of farmers.

Walking along the straight roads, Rig came to a hall, the doors looked south, a fine outlook. Pushed to was the door, a ring set in the post. He entered the airy, rush-strewn room.

In he stepped; there sat the couple, Father and Mother, busy with their fingers, yet attentive to each other, looking straight into each others' eyes. Father, a strong vigorous, intelligent man, twisted bow-strings, bent elm, shaped arrows. The lady was admiring the arms of her dress, stroking the material, straightening the sleeves. Her head-dress was set

69

straight, there was a pendant on her breast, a short, full cape
and a blue-stitched blouse; her brow was brighter, her breast
more shining, her neck was whiter than freshly-fallen snow.

Well knew Rig	wisely to counsel;
on middle seat	he sate him down,
betwixt the twain	of the toft benched him.

Mother took an embroidered tablecloth of white linen,
covered the table, then she brought a fine loaf of white flour,
and put it on the cloth. She set out full dishes chased with
silver, pork and bacon, roast game. There was wine in the
cups, fine ornamented goblets. They drank and revelled as
the day drew to a close, then up Rig rose, got ready for bed;
'Betwixt the twain of the toft he laid him'. There he was for
three nights together, before he passed on.

Nine moons passed; Mother gave birth to a boy, swathed
him in silk, poured water over him, named him Lord. Bright
was his hair, bright his cheeks, piercing were his eyes, like a
young snake's.

Lord grew up in that hall. He began to brandish shields,
fit bow strings, bend the elm bow, shape arrows, hurl spears,
ride horses, swim, hunt with hounds, wield a sword.

Then came Rig walking one day, stepping out of a
thicket. Rig taught him runes, gave him his own name, declared
him as his son. Then he told him to get ancestral property,
the *othal*, to establish a settlement, to conquer.

Lord rode through the dark wood, over the frost-covered
mountains, until he came to a hall. He hurled his shafted spear,
brandished his linden shield. He started a war, reddened the
plains with blood; dead men fell, he fought for that land. He
alone then ruled many settlements. He began to use his wealth,
offered to everyone gifts, treasures and trinkets and lean-
ribbed horses, squandered he the wealth he took by force of
arms, hacked up arm-rings to give to his comrades.

Messengers came over the dewy roads, came to the hall where Chieftain lived. There lived the slender-fingered girl, radiant and wise; they called her Erna. The betrothal party asked for her hand and home they drove her, married her to Lord; she wore the bridal veil. They lived together, loved one another, raised a clan and enjoyed their lives.

Son was their eldest, and Child the second, Youth and Noble, Heir and Offspring, Descendant and Kinsman, Sonny and Lad. They swam together and played at *tafl*, the game of strategy. Lineage one was called, Kon, the young King, was the youngest.

Lord's children grew up there, tamed horses, brandished shields, practised shooting, used ash spears. But King, young Kon the youngest boy alone knew runes, runes eternal and runes of life, ageless runes, and runes of mystery. He knew how to help in childbirth, deaden sword-blades, quiet the ocean. He understood birds' speech, quenched fires, pacified and quietened men, made sorrows disappear, had the strength and vigour of eight men.

The time came when he contended in rune-wisdom with his father, Rig the Earl; Kon it was who knew more tricks. Thus he gained and got the right to be called Rig; and more, he gained runic lore.

Young Kon rode through woods and thickets, shooting bird arrows, charming down the birds. Then a crow spoke from its branch - 'Why, young Kon, are you killing birds? Rather you ought to be riding horses, conquering armies. Your kinsmen Dan and Danp have better houses and fairer lands than you hold; well they know the ship's keel to ride, the sword to wield and wounds to strike."

The poem leaves us where Kon, who is now called Rig, is poised at the brink of maturity. He is the most learned man in the world, and now the challenge – from the old crow – comes to action, to conquest. Will he follow the taunting of the crow, and conquer more than any other man? Yes, because he is named as King.

Yet, somehow, in our day and age, the tale comes down to us incomplete, apparently; a fable which could go either way, if we wanted it to; and what is a sorcerer, a runemaster such as Kon, if not a man who examines every route through life, in order to find the one that is uniquely his? The poem does not tell us what Kon's decision is, back then in the version written down in the aftermath of the Viking Age, but this old tale I believe would have had different endings in different eras. And strange endings might suit our strange age...

The Return Of Rig

Lord Heimdall strode out one bright Spring morning, over the Rainbow bridge. He had the leisure to revisit an old concern of his, having paid some dwarves to create a tiny kink in time, during which his absence would not be noticed by any of the enemies of Asgard. He passed through the veil of spun opal sparkling with traceries of rare stellar isotopes, all suspended in a shimmering web of Dark-Elf magic. He stepped through into Midgard. He had come to visit his progeny, the children bred from his divine being.

Striding straight down the roads of an ancient city built by his people, his heart was as buoyant as ever. First, he decided to visit the descendants of Thrall, the farm-slave. His super-senses see and hear many of these men and women toiling in the fields the world over, working as simple farm labourers. But in this changed world, he saw many of Thrall's heirs in strange circumstances. A god who has a strong instinct for trouble, Rig decided to investigate.

The magic of his being guided him effortlessly. He found himself in a damp, dark valley between tall buildings, entering a set of quiet streets. The world seemed colourless, washed-out, poor on detail, low in reality tone. As Rig passed, things lit up and acquired sudden depth, detail, colour. Bricks developed russet highlights, trees bloomed.

The silence here was not of peace, but of paralysis. Rig stepped up to a house, the door closed tight. His magical presence, the *hamingja* of a god, caused the door to just swing open. The room was almost empty. A floor of some synthetic fibre; two dirty armchairs; a couple, the man rangy and dirty, the woman cleaner, but with cross eyes, they sat under a harsh electric light, watching a talking dumb show in a box of sour blueish light. Rig smiled; the scene was not so unfamiliar: Thrall and his woman, keeping house. Rig sat down on their settee. His authority focussed them, and they joined him, one on either side. The TV set turned itself off. This time, Rig had come not to advise; more to assimilate.

They set before him this marvelous industrial food, irradiated with dwarf rays and served in shining thin metal. Rig knew that its nutritional value was negligible, most of its value coming from the design on the packet and its associated mythology.

Rig drank in the world of these people. They would never in any society rise above the level of immediate material gratification; they would build nothing new, only survive and prosper in their own way. Just as they had all these centuries, the same as ever. Rig touched them gently, with the reserve of a loving, clever god, leaving them with enhanced luck, for their sweet hospitality. He walked on down the city streets, proud and brisk. It was not his business to change the world that men had built.

He went looking for the kin of Farmer. His method of looking was that of a god who can hear and see anything in the world. He went and sat down in a pretty little park in the great city and fed the birds, their observant and informative chatter a familiar background to the vast field of data he processed in his mind. All the sounds of the world were his to tune into, all the sights too... his eyes rolled weirdly in their sockets, his vision rotating through impossible angles as swarms of data were gathered and extrapolated, lives unfolding their narratives from the chaos of impressions. He saw practitioners of dwarf technologies, building weapons and medicines and data machines. He saw many traders, he saw tally-men, who counted piles of make-believe gold tokens. Something fell into place: These people were like dwarves - the world was being run by men who modelled themselves on Dark Elves! Much became clear. The whole place smelt like Svartalfheim's furnaces, rich with exotic poisons from the smelting of rare ores... Men should not have to live like this, but this seems to be what those in power had chosen.

Some unexpected shifts had occurred: Farmer's class had bred teachers, doctors, lawyers – but with the acquisitive values of their true class. Rig's curiosity was piqued by the vast wealth some Farmers had accumulated. Did the Farmers now run the world? Certainly, if anyone did these days, they didn't have much of a clue as to how to do it. Rig decided to investigate at first hand. His ear picked out the roar of a private plane overhead: Farmer's Lear jet back from grouse-shooting in Scotland.

He walked down the broad streets, and found the Farmers' city residence. The hostel was grandiose, with a less privileged one of Farmer's descendants securing the door. Rig had some advice for him. His response to this made it easy for Rig to enter. When he reached the Farmers' penthouse, the door was open. A strong, stiff man in the prime of life was trying to relax in the foam of a shell-shaped jacuzzi. A phone and a laptop computer lay by the bath. The man was attended by a beautiful young woman, naked except for a gold chain round her slender waist, who soaped him and poured into his ear a stream of barbed gossip. Farmer and his wife, keeping house. Rig, being a god, was welcomed warmly into their home. 'What do gods eat?', Mrs. Farmer inquired, with no real disrespect. Rig smiled and said: 'Whatever delights you'. The lady of the house had dismissed the servants, anticipating a rare night of sexual indulgence with her busy husband. She laid the table with a fine linen cloth, and set out silver dishes and crystal wine glasses. They sat down to a sumptuous and refined meal, brought in by a caterer's employee, another Farmer descendant of lower status.

They ate and drank as the light faded in the city sky. Rig had no advice for them, but on the impulse of a mature god, he left them with a vision of the totality of life. Not in the cruel way you might imagine, as a demonic reflection of the emptiness of a driven existence, but by way of enhancing their sheer pleasure in the moment. Let them feel what it really is to be alive.

Rig strode on down the straight roads, breathing high, loving every minute of it. He found himself back at the little park, and sat under a tree, scanning the world, gigabytes flickered through his incredible senses, that could hear grass grow, the wool sprouting on the backs of sheep. He had seen that the underclass, as they were now known, were unchanged, just materially better off for a while, at least until the time he had to blow the Gjallahorn and announce the Ragnarok. The Farmers – they had got this world sewn up in their money-bags. The warrior class too seemed little changed, other than having become infected with the slave-religions, albeit in a muscular form acceptable to warriors. The warriors now served the system set up by the Farmers.

As for what should be the rulers, those who lead from the front, they just don't seem to exist! What have they become? It was tribal leaders before the days of Dan and Danpr, then those two and the foundation of kingdoms. Then the brutal and often stupid aristocracy that ruled the Roman empire, and its successor via the christian warrior cults of Northern Europe, the British. That in turn had grown away from its centre and fallen, leaving a world ruled by commerce.

What had become of the estate of the Earls, the Lords, those who had united the tribes through conquest, spawning the great King, the young Kon?

His mind turned to the most powerful and divided of the Lord clan: Since he was the nurturer of the spark of intelligence, he rejoiced in the boy Kon, whom he taught the runes to. He had left the youth in the paradox of a sorcerer: should he get involved in the struggles of the world, or pursue the more hidden mysteries of life and death and magical power? He followed the possible strands of the Kon tale forward...

Kon had been living in the woods, having found his own place where he could live quietly, primitive, alone and totally free. He could best any man, and is a fine sorcerer, a God indeed. He had the leisure of an animal at the top of the food-chain, a super-intelligent animal. The words of the crow drew him back into human intercourse, which for most people means Law, Compromise: the Human Condition. Maybe not for such a mighty man as Kon. He saw runes in bent leaves, in shadows on the bark of a fallen silver birch, our Lady high and bright, almost phosphorescent pearling light in the forest shade, dappling cracks patterning the bark, making messages to him...

Kon had reached the apex of development of his magical skills, but was still acting like a boy, still learning. But something starts him out of his woodland retreat, with names that begin with daylight, his powerful brothers. A young man with the sap rising in him, he begins to desire a mate, a bright, spirited, lusty girl to love... maybe this is what sets him on the path of conquest. Her white arms tease him through the glades and shade and light and dapple... He comes half-to on his bed of moss, her hair whispering on his cheek as he wakes, his nostrils full of her fragrance, like the scent of a pale yellow wood he has no name for... Who is she, whose name darts in trails of runes changing too fast to read?

A god now, he can give himself advice; he moves out one morning, following the scent of the daybreak, into a world waiting for him to make his mark on it. He knows the one desire he has, and that is all he needs to polarize him into action. His horse snorts steam in the crisp spring morning. Hills roll down from a vantage point made for a god: streaming light over fields of green. His world.

And he made a kingdom, and met his girl, and married her, and they loved each other... And that tale is not at all for here, because it twists and turns more than any other story ever told. In any case, they gave birth to mighty heirs, kings of the world, monsters and geniuses.

Rig asked himself whether there could be another great King today. No, the world could not take it any more; there was nowhere left to conquer. With no conquest, there must be another way to renew the world. He scanned some more, looking for reputation; acres of data scrolled through his eyes, all assimilated in lightning flashes by his superhuman awareness, ears that can hear the echoes of words spoken a thousand years ago, eyes that can fetch back the shards of light that have crossed the starry void.

He searched for the true aristocrats, the elder kin of the house of Jarl. He found royals who are no longer truly aristocratic, debilitated and warped by christianity or wallowing in decadence, spending their energy on intoxication and shopping. Like the disinherited they were irrelevant to Rig's quest. He scanned for the true traces of nobility in other humans.

Among the data streams he found some individuals who stood out; some the descendants of Kon, his own descendants, some from other ancient and kingly lineages of other folk. He focussed his search through the lens of the high values of Lord's people; strange connections came up in front of him: an army officer, a warrior who fought for his people courageously, and as justly as is possible in the course of a war, and was court-martialled for his daring honesty; a writer who satirized mediocrity all his life, only to be arse-licked by the establishment that had once hated him; a dead music star renowned for extraordinarily elite manners. True strands of nobility were rare enough; where their influence was more than marginal in this rotten society was harder to discern.

Rig rubbed his chin, a mighty god meditating on the strangeness of the way that things necessarily worked out.

Yes, this was a society run by tally-men. The wizards of the world: what influence had they held, and what did they hold now? Rig reflected how the heirs of Kon had always been responsible for great transformations of society. Scanning back again through the echoing galleries of the years, he came across souls who had exhibited that strange genius. Knowing now what human signs he sought, he stood up and walked.

The young man, Neil King, was sitting on a bench in the little park, watching the birds, charming them down. Rig approached him. In a flash, he read all of the man's past. Without further ado, they engaged in conversation. King opened his heart, and said how he felt a great sense of loss, of wasted potential. He remembered his youthful enthusiasm for the Work, his devotion to magic. The taunts of his contemporaries, and infinitely worse, his own doubts which drove him away from his path, into the pursuit of material wealth. Then at a time when everyone seemed to be accumulating cash, he had begun to realise his own strange nature, and had resumed his magical work. King invited Rig back to his apartment. He busied himself preparing a meal for the god.

Neil King placed the final course on the table. Rig asked: "What is it you wish to tell me about this food?"

He faced Rig. "I stole the cream".

Rig was able to give him some good advice: "Theft can make a slave of you, O nobly-born. Robbery is more honourable" His voice was grave and resonant, and he smiled broadly. Neil served him a portion of the rich dessert, looking him straight in the eye.

As they finished their meal, Rig turned to Neil and spoke: "Be prepared to lose everything you have."

Then he rose and without a look behind, strode to the door. King followed him. They left the building, and Rig led them back through the city night to the area of the neo-Thralls, shrouded in electric darkness now. They entered the warren of dull lanes, now uniformly yellow under the streetlights, and Rig found what he was looking for. She stood by a long industrial wall, four streets radiating from her forming her escape routes. She wore high heels and a thin, flimsy dress of bright red. They approached her. She was in her late teens, with short, colourful hair and eyes that held memories of weapons and despair. Rig spoke: 'Be ready to gain more than you can imagine'. She looked at Rig, impressed but not englamoured. She nodded and said in a low, clear voice 'Dyra'.

Back at his home, Neil brought a crystal flagon of golden mead to the table. He poured it into a glass and offered it to Rig, who took a draught, and passed it to Dyra. There was a breathless silence as they drank.

They sat close but not touching, the humans' nerves buzzing and arcing with the touch of the god's breath. Rig had seldom seen such calm devotion, such commitment to the moment of communion. The mead had become a sacred elixir. For an hour or so, the time of clocks softly receding into the background, they monitored their breathing, wobbling up into the flesh-transforming trance, the first seith trance, the trance that heals. Rig was aware of the next plateau forming a few minutes later, as they opened to the trance that dissolves reality itself. They all stood up together and went into the soft, dark bedroom.

Rig stayed there for three days. Not because any law required it, but because he wanted to. Rig could not help but love people. He is their protector, the guarantor of guardianship, and the guardian himself of the Rainbow Bridge, the narrow and terrible direct route to ecstasy for the brave few, and for the Gods. Of course he loved people; his was not a scrupulous fair-mindedness, a representation of impartial values, but a passionate love, and like all passionate loves, did not have to belong to any overall plan as perceived by any but the lover, and if he be blessed, the beloved. In other words, he did not need to be consistent; his love was his truth. As was his nature, he enjoyed the Slave family, and the more civilized Farmer couple. But the nights with Neil and Dyra were a work of alchemy. That work showed these people as the apex of the unnatural development of the human spirit.

The three days were a mighty work of magic, turning the great wheels of Time. Rig's seed was a pearl dropped in their overlapping minds as they climaxed, a black sun that shattered, refracted and recombined all the elements of time, so that the possible futures became penetrable, and the terrifying arcade of infinite worlds opened to their gaze.

The pearl flared, blazing indigo, as it twisted itself out of the four dimensions, boiling its essence off into the spectral wave-space of Bifrost, salting the colours of the rainbow bridge in a morning never imagined.

For a brief moment, the God-wave held its breath, and then surged out around the planet in a shock-front of pure illumination to the sorcerous kin of Kon, those humans who could withstand its terrible power, who had individuated enough for their minds not to be consumed by the presence of the living god.

On he strode, in the middle of the roads, his heart buoyant as ever in his fierce love for people, especially the really interesting ones. At some point he stepped onto the roads that, amongst men, are known only to the kin of Kon the sorcerer-king, the true Lords of the Earth.

Back in Asgard, Heimdall ran some emulations: he ran the stories of Kon's bloodline, back to the beginning. He saw that all Kon's people, all the sorcerers, are on a cusp of decision, and that this cusp is not trivial, that these are the people that do actually have free will: they are the creators of novelty in the universe, being profoundly dissatisfied with what is, once they learn what can be.

And then he ran it fast, to the end of all songs, the probable Ragnarok of this whole great cycle. Kon's descendants are the heirs to a transmuted universe. They are the ones who are capable of sustaining consciousness and ecstasy, throughout eternity. They are the prototypes of a new kind of immortal.

Rig's final mask fell away, revealing behind the self that loves humanity the pure intelligence of Odhr, the one Eye that blazes at the core of all consciousness.

1 All quotes in this chapter from Lee M. Hollander's translation of *The Poetic Edda*.

Dwarf-spirit for healthy pursuits and lifestyle

Chapter 7
A Modern Magician and the Northern Tradition

Whatever lineages of magical instruction existed before christianity, they are long lost, with the possible exception of a few rural traditions. Without an initiatic lineage, how do we rate our prowess at magic? We have to evaluate our development through the practical results we create.

This pragmatic approach has its most developed form in chaos magic. Sometimes the sceptical, results-based discipline of that magical path leads to a misunderstanding: that chaos magic is only about 'doing spells or sigils' for personal gain. Opening up the question of why we attempt magic leads us to a deeper understanding. Although magic is, practically by definition, a path of power, surely we do not do it solely for the effects we can make on the world. We cannot rely on magic as a substitute for more worldly skills. Our ancestors knew this. In *The Lay of Fafnir*, a poem of the *Elder Edda*, Sigurd says:

> The Helm of Awe protects no-one
> where angry men have to fight;

I think a shrewd guess may tell us that individuals who went into battle armed only with a powerful sigil took a rapid, Darwinian route to extinction.

No: the effects we have on the world are, or should be, useful to us. But they point to more than themselves. They can be taken as signs that we are on the right track. But that leaves the question: Towards what?

My personal answer to the question, the urge that got me into magic, was: To find something to assuage the abiding sense that materialist dogma produces of having been robbed or defrauded. There was a slogan going round in my youth which summed this awareness up nicely: *Reality is a rip-off*. Part of the price we pay for the wonders of industrial culture is a scientistic dogma which aggressively contends that only *things* are really real. Only exterior surfaces are worth investigating. All depth, all interiority, all subjective experience is denied or denigrated as a mere epiphenomenon, a sideshow, of matter. So I sought a way to take me beyond the prison planet of materialism, to prove my subjective connection to the universe, so as to re-enchant the universe in my own eyes.

Now, there are many agendas that seek or claim to assuage this emptiness. To a naturally skeptical person such as myself, there are few believable options.

We may at first seek to reintroduce magic by the retro-romantic ploy. The history of various forms of romantic escapism resonate through the modern era. We take on such a sweet deceiver and we may get a few days, or weeks, or even months of naïve belief, of magical puppy-love, before it wears thin, and the critical faculties come back into play. That ploy then succeeds only in showing us what we *want* reality to be like, rather than convincing us that it is actually like that.

Beyond retro-romanticism we have Postmodernism; we can let a chink of light into the prison: we are allowed to doubt that there is only one valid description of reality. We are no longer stuck with the narrowest interpretation of the materialist Aeon. The world is now full of guerrilla ontologies.

Under this tolerant regime, guerilla spirituality may flourish, and, just as every coin has two sides, the desperate search for some spiritual dimension outside of mainstream religion has two main forms: the mass movement known as the New Age and the tiny band of dedicated people who call themselves by the old-fashioned and deservedly romantic name of magicians.

PostModernism allows such a romantic position, without treating it as ludicrous, unlike a 4th Aeon/ Materialist critique would. But on closer inspection, PoMo isn't *really* magic-friendly at all; it simply tolerates all universe-maps. It's a philosophy that can't say no. It opens the door to all comers, but has nowhere in particular for the guests to stand, let alone sit, since it refuses to privilege any one viewpoint over any other. Its tolerance merely includes, without truly utilizing. And, because of its refusal to privilege any one view, it cannot distinguish the genuine from the false or corrupt. In the roadside diner of Postmodernism, magic may be on the menu, but the diners are as likely to be served the uncritical slop known as new age (or, as I prefer to call it, for the rhyme, 'newage') as they are the nourishment of real wisdom.

The Newager wants instant faith without thought, just like the faiths of previous Aeons offer.

In contrast, in order to convince anyone who is sophisticated in 4th Aeon thought – i.e. anyone who's been exposed to science and thought about what it actually means – the evidence required is that some real, material, consensually-visible change occur in conformity with our individual Will.

With chaos magic we demand such tough evidence for our mind's involvement with cosmic processes.

Chaos magic is capable of demonstrating to each practitioner that, with sufficient precision and passion, you can use pretty much any belief to dance with the universe.

85

What Counts As Magic?

So what counts as magic? What counts as personal proof that I am connected to the universe? My short answer is: weirdness.

I have twelve anecdotes to present to you, of increasing levels of peculiarness. They're spread over thirty years of magical practice.

Anecdote 1. The scene: A large group ritual in a mixed-background magical group in the English Midlands. A broadside of 'gnostic techniques' have been used over a few hours, and the climactic working is a healing, for a group member who has had an inflamed bowel which has recently got much worse.

For the healing, I am to do a kind of psychic surgery, extracting the magical form of the disease and neutralizing it. After a struggle, the working was totally successful. My friend had a rather scary crisis later that night, then recovered completely, from a syndrome she'd had for ten years.

That was over ten years ago, and apparently the syndrome never came back.

Anecdote 2. The scene is a big public meeting in the USA, one month before 9-11. My friend assists at a fire-ritual and gets burned. Some of the group rush her to hospital, and her right arm is treated for 1st and 2nd degree burns (we're not talking magical grades here, but degrees of tissue damage).

In a magical device called a chaotron, a convoluted pattern of human energies and breath, the exact shape of which is synchronistically divined by at least three people, we all pour healing energy into her. The doctor has said that she won't be able to do without a dressing for two weeks, but in twenty-four hours she was able to remove

In a magical device called a *chaotron*, a convoluted pattern of human energies and breath, the exact shape of which is synchronistically divined by at least 3 people, we all pour healing energy into her. The doctor has said that she won't be able to do without a dressing for two weeks, but in 24 hours she was able to remove the bandages, and a day later the burns had healed without trace.

Anecdote 3. A magical group meeting in London. I present a ritual for remote healing. We have heard that our friend and magical associate has just been diagnosed with massive kidney damage. He has lost two thirds of his kidney function. We use a completely absent procedure, the magical link being some hair in a wax doll. We use a dark voudon-style invocation, of the Zaraguin loa, the spider lords of the future and nanotechnology. Why, for a healing? Because they're damned impressive, and also stop any other entities getting the energy.

Result: at next measurement, a few days later, the specialist declares that he now has recovered one of the lost thirds of his kidney function. Our friend quotes him as saying: 'I don't know what you're doing, but keep doing it!'

Definition A:

So, looking at those three successes, we have a first layer of weirdness. I call it **Body Alchemy**. These effects are apparently caused by action of will entirely within the skin, or involving recordable, non-occult communication between skin-bounded humans.

This is what psychologists might call a holistic-psychological effect. There is actually nothing here to challenge materialistic scientism. The will acts via some subconscious instructions to change gene expression. This type of causality includes firewalking, wart-charming, most forms of healing and the so-called placebo effect, which is, of course, healing magic.

Despite the impressiveness of some of the effects in this area, it could be said that this isn't really magic at all, because science can, with an increasingly small stretch, explain it. The finding that immune system cells communicate with central nervous system sites was one of the discoveries that narrowed the gap and enabled more materialistic scientists to take the plunge of believing in psychosomatic healing.

This explanation will work for anecdotes 1 and 2. The person was there whilst people were physically communicating with them in both cases.

It can also serve for anecdote 3. Since the target person knew the ritual was being performed for him, it could have catalyzed a shift of belief massive enough to do that impressive bit of healing on his kidneys.

To be more generous with our belief, we could regard that third healing as weak evidence for a transpersonal, telepathic effect of some kind, as well as body alchemy. The following examples are, I think, stronger evidence for some effect of that kind.

Anecdote 4. An Initiation Rite in a chaos magic group, outdoors in the Yorkshire hills. At one point I am one of the members that has the task of hurling psychic patterns at the candidate, by way of challenge and disorientation. I see a flash of something, intensely, momentarily and memorably. Later, I draw it and show it round. One of our members shows me a drawing of a sigil which he had been projecting, which is exactly the same.

Anecdote 5. At the Barbican Centre, listening to a concert performance of Wagner's *Walküre*. I feel a sudden pain in my back, so I shift my position and ignore it. A couple of weeks later, during an innner voyage, I realize that I am running an abuse trauma, and that it isn't mine. I trace it back to that pain in the back at the concert, and succeed in digging it out and rejecting it.

Definition B:

These events show effects which are not confined to the skin. I'll label this effect **Transpersonal,** meaning that instructions and other information appear to be transferred between two or more people's nervous systems.

As an aside, I think this level fits the reality of Astrology as I observe it: it seems to have a weak effect, not enough for accurate predictions, but enough to generate a fairly consistent set of zodiacal types. I think it works at this weak level not because of radiations from the stars, but because of expectations generated by unconscious acceptance of its myth. Sun-sign typing provides a myth to explain the fact that we are all different, but fall into certain archetypal roles in our interactions with each other. People pick this up unconsciously, maybe because of other people's expectations of their behaviour – Oh, he's born in November, treat him like a Scorpio – but I think it more likely that we soak up the whole mythos telepathically, and sculpt our behaviour accordingly from an early age. We fall into a limited number of archetypal roles on the stage of life, ready-made off the peg identities generated by the mythos of astrology.

The next two anecdotes provide stronger evidence of some transpersonal effect, and also for something beyond that.

Anecdote 6. A friend and magical co-worker, wrongly accused and persecuted by some bizarre obsession of the authorities, is advised by his lawyer to plead guilty. He rejects this advice and comes to me to help him with some magical work, to take his case to Crown Court and get a full acquittal. A few months before, we had been among the creators of a mega-servitor, the kind of egregore-entity that carries the power of a whole magical group. We turn this beast loose on the courtroom and instruct it to get my friend acquitted. I accompany him into court, to help keep the critter powered up, and shall never forget the happy, serene look on the Judge's face as he makes the summing up. Basically, he tells the jury to ignore the probably dubious attestations of the police and extend their sympathy to the plight of my friend. Against his lawyer's expectations, he is acquitted.

Anecdote 7. This next incident was not one of my own successes, but I include it because it is so stunning. My friend had lost touch with a friend of hers. All she knew was that he lived in York. So, to get a phone number for him, she took her tarot deck and drew six cards. Being new to magic, she was overwhelmed by the idea of the sheer weirdness of what success might mean. So, she left it a day before phoning the number she'd got. The number turned out to be that of the next door neighbour of my friend's friend.

Definition C:

Here, we seem to be looking at something which not only suggests communication between nervous systems, but some kind of coordination of effects between more than two nervous systems. One of the definitions of magic I like is by Pete Carroll: *the engineering of synchronicities.* So I'd label these anecdotes as **Strong Transpersonal** and also as **Synchronistic.** With such results, it seems as if the world is a matrix, or an operating system, or a field of interconnected consciousnesses.

The two examples I just gave show this connection as still recognizably tied to human brains, albeit in a way which science cannot explain, only reject. Some experiences take us even beyond this, where the non-human world itself seems to be affected by our magic. This next example has just that quality.

Anecdote 8. I and 3 friends are trying out a new pathworking, Pete Carroll's Cthonos. We decide to go for a very precise, publicly-visible result, the BBC 9 o'clock news having a problem on sound sufficiently serious to warrant an apology from the newsreader, between 9.10 and 9.15. We sit down for this quiet, inward working, when a burglar alarm goes off in the bakery next door. We delay the start for a while, then decide that if we are going to do the working before the news starts, we have to just get on with it. So we sit there for about twenty minutes doing our visualization with this shrill screaming in our ears. When we finish, we rush down and get the news on just as it is starting. We get our result at 9.12. It's one of the most precise magical results I've ever had.

Definition D:

This seems to be a *strong Synchronistic* effect, only partially dependent on a human brain receiving the information my group put out there. This is what is commonly thought-of as being magic: events with no apparent physical connection bend the rules of probability; effects occur as if will acts directly on the physical universe, without the intermediary of a human receiver. Remote viewing is another effect of this kind.

Stronger examples of such effects are in the next two anecdotes.

Anecdote 9. On this occasion, a group of us are asked to do an exorcism for a couple in Sheffield. Now, the deal is, that the people who set up the investigation are film students from Manchester Film College and insist on a film team being present. So our group decide to make it a group research event, and four of us tramp over to a middle-class housing estate on the ring road to meet with the agreed minimum of two filmmakers. To cut a long and educational story short, we end up looking at a piece of video film which confirms the description of the main hauntee, whom we incidentally decide was the source of the hauntings. He had told us he experienced the entities that were vampirizing his girlfriend as wrapping themselves around his neck like sleepy cats. Our video shows clearly a band of smoky light around his neck like a scarf on two sequences.

I count this as an evocation to visible appearance.

Anecdote 10. Right back at the beginning of my magical career, I lived in a house which some people said had a strong, occasionally somewhat unpleasant spirit in it. After various unsuccessful attempts to banish it, my girlfriend and I finally succeed, as confirmed by visitors the next day, with an energetic bout of sex magic. As we finish, we hear an unfamiliar noise, as if it was raining in the house. The rain is the water from a burst main hitting the cellar ceiling and spraying down.

Definition E:

Here, we seem to have direct effects on matter itself. OK, the exorcism video could be interpreted as a local electromagnetic field around the guy's neck, which would drop the weirdness level back to something like body alchemy, but I believe it's worth including here because of the close fit with the hauntee's description of it. The burst pipe incident indicates a much higher level of energy transfer than that. We are looking at some crossover of **Synchronistic** effects, as outlined above, with what is usually called an **Etheric** effect.

The final two anecdotes are examples of stronger effects of this kind.

Anecdote 11. I had a very interesting few months' runup to my Invocation of the Holy Guardian Angel working Goetia with a talented and eccentric group in the Midlands. Settling down for a night of demonic jaunts, five of us occupied a large rope circle in a room over a pub in central Birmingham.

We had three demons on the menu that night, this being the climax of three months' workings. The first two gave little trouble. Then our Master of the Temple got his particular spirit focused in the Triangle of evocation, and the weird stuff started. We had the classic drop in temperature, and a more impressive event: Our MT had been sitting cross-legged at the edge of the circle, facing the Triangle. His weapon of Will was a purbah, a large, Tibetan-style brass dagger, which was about six feet away from him within the circle. At some point in his negotiation with the demon, things started getting sticky, and he reached for the purbah. With no perceptible pause, the dagger was no longer six feet away, but in his hand. All five of us witnessed this.

Now for the weirdest of all.

Anecdote 12. Back near the beginning of my magical career, my lover was a woman of extreme psychic ability, whom I shall refer to as Anna for the purpose of this tale. This person it was who, one afternoon when I went round to visit her during a light summer storm, was standing in her kitchen shaking, lightning having just come through her window and struck her washing machine. On another occasion, she and I were at the home of another magician. She started telling a story about how her ex-boyfriend had been a little peeved when she got into his sports car and it blew up. The TV which had been on in the background emitted strangled noises and gouts of sparks and ceased working for ever.

Anyway, one evening, after a meeting where we've been doing pathworkings, four of us are sitting around back at Anna's place. We're drinking nothing stronger than tea, and the conversation had faded into an easy, pleasant late-night silence. Then, looking up I noticed that Anna, who'd been lying on the floor, was now raised off it. It seemed that only the back of her head was touching the carpet, and the rest of her was upwards, straight, at an angle of about 30⁰ to the horizontal. Her left hand was raised to touch her brow, as if she was concentrating. This image stayed perfectly in focus, unlike fleeting eidetic input from the deep mind. I looked round at the other two witnesses, who looked as silently awed as I was. After a few seconds, Anna was flat on the floor again, and I asked her what she'd experienced. She replied that she had felt herself drift upwards, just as all three observers had witnessed.

It is worth adding that everyone was sober, and at that stage, that was our norm.

This can only be explained as a **Strong Etheric** effect, something acting directly on the material world. This is also the realm of poltergeist activity. We have here what appears to be an outright violation of normal physical constraints. We are definitely no longer in Kansas, or even any official version of Leeds. This kind of thing, a dogmatic materialist can only consign to the abyss of unrespectable, anecdotal evidence – the realm of *the Damned*, as Charles Fort called it.

Belief and Gnosis

So through those experiences, amongst many others, I sought and succeeded in proving to myself that, at the very least, the universe is a lot weirder place than science gives it credit for. One reason for doing magic is satisfied. However, we are left with a problem.

The Chaos Magic approach can be done naively – without any critical appreciation of the belief structures used. This leaves the practitioner open to accusations of mall-shopping superficiality in their paradigm-hopping, and sometimes people accuse chaos magicians of just that.

That aside there is a real problem with the technology of belief. We have an uneasy compromise going on here – if we do magic to change and re-enchant the universe, then we are seeking a change of belief, but belief itself is devalued by demonstrating its relativity. When our magic uses belief as a technique, then belief cannot help orientate us in the world. It cannot provide a centre for the chaos magician. So what can?

The two features of the core technology that has come to be called chaos magic are belief and gnosis, or what I call ESCs – extraordinary states of consciousness.

It is the very extraordinariness of gnosis that releases us from the trap of postmodernism, by being a privileged state. Whilst Chaos magic is as non-hierarchical a theory of magic as has ever been put forward, attempts to reduce magic to a total postmodernist flatland are doomed to fail, because of the necessity to privilege the state we call gnosis above ordinary states. Magic will always have an element of rebellion against the flatland aspect of PostModernism, and whilst belief cannot, ultimately, change us, the practice of magic and gnosis can and will. We have regained the occasional ability to perform miracles, and the mental tools we use to do so free us from conditioned identity.

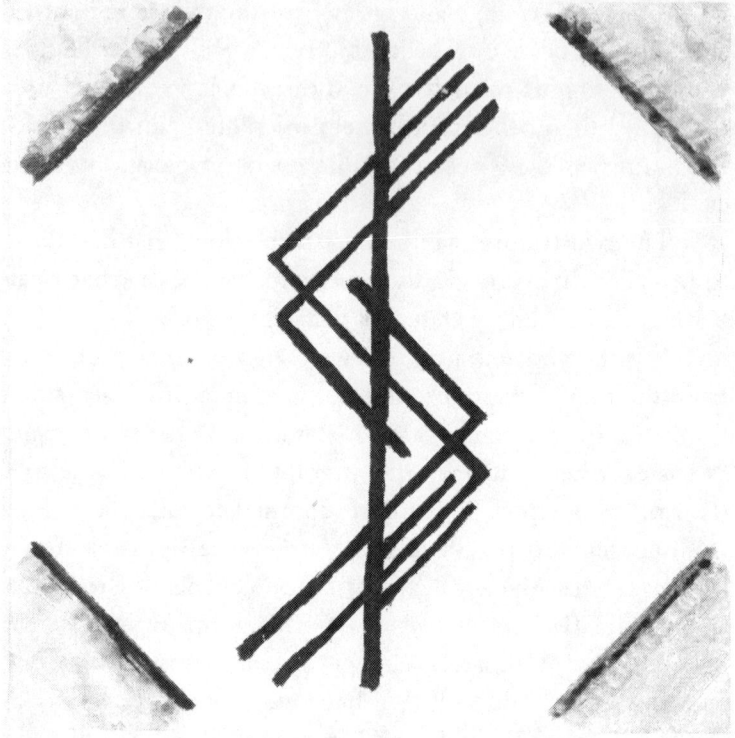

Dwarf-spirit for investment

Chapter 8
The City Eats Us

Even at its most orderly, a city of eight million people is deeply chaotic; in such a galaxy of human beings, a universe of possibilities arises each day. On top of this, there is the memory of the city itself, etched in bricks and roads, grime and traffic, a palimpsest of dreams and desires, images and obsessions. The city's memory is a realm of criminals and heroes, legends and gods; and the city's inhabitants, to a greater or lesser degree, feel themselves to be players on the city's stage, characters and maybe narrators, in a timeless, engulfing story.

For this mythic nourishment we pay a price. The city eats us. I know this, because I come from outside of it, from a place where all but the most ancient traces of human life are scoured away by the wind, eroded by the silence. I can see the city's mechanisms; I can see how the system works. I can see the bargains that humans strike with things that are bigger than them – a story, a myth, a news report; things that lend their brief lives a dimension of eternity. Because the weirdest things that people do are all in some way attempts to overcome their death.

So this is a story I can tell because I know these people, this group of friends and enemies, and I know the eight things they tried to do to each other and the world around them using magical power. My name is Luke Slaithwaite, and you'll have a tough time pronouncing that. My story is short, and will not detain you long from your bus journey, your train, your meeting.

Here they are, these friends, in an upstairs pub room, a pagan moot, drinking the draught that wipes away the exhaustion of the city.

First off, we have Bob, forty-something, slim, and mercurial. He luxuriates in the dense human jungle as he holds court, pint in hand, telling a joke to his usual gallery of admirers. In his pocket he jingles a keyring, accumulating energy into a spell for more power, more luck and more women. He likes to be generous. Typical quote: *My round!*

Here is Jeanette, tall and queenly, in a rustic cotton dress with a soft silk scarf at her throat. She is the author of a definitive volume on Egyptian magic and has been Bob's wife for five years. She and Bob have a turbulent marriage, and it's going through one of its rougher passages right now. Jeanette appreciates focus, concentration and careful analysis, and her typical quote might be: *Can't you think more quietly?*

Now we see Timothy, bookish, intense, with mysterious depths. He has just arrived on a Docklands Light Railway train from south of the river, reading a book about the Beaker People's sacred vessels, grooved with the entoptic patterns of psychedelic vision. He gazed outwards at the entoptic cityscape, the perfect repeating windows of Canary Wharf blurring into pure pattern, patterns from within the mind brought out into the world. He has been in love with dark, slender Jeannette for years. He has just come from working on a magic painting. His iPod plays one of his painting soundtracks, and he listens intently to the perfection of The Shadows again. *Wonderful Land* rises from the first high phrases, so much yearning compressed so precisely into a mere melody, an immortal tune. The guitar soars into a misty-eyed reverie, its solid luminosity becoming translucent and wobbly with tremolo, then its helpless bliss borne passively aloft by the rising strings. The reaching-up of the sound brings on his vision of a hundred mirrors, Jeanette's face in every one, his painter's hand telling the beads of an infinite mala for his remote Goddess. His typical quote is from a 2004 Honda advert: '*Hate something / Change something / Hate is a good thing*'

Here's Neil, blond dreads cascading past a pretty face with high cheekbones. He has come straight from a restaurant launch just off Regent's Street. Licking the rich terrine off his fingertips, he notices the black smear there. He remembers how the train had been crowded, and he'd rested his hand on a shelf over a notice that said KEEP CLEAR. As he'd withdrawn it, it had left a thick stain down the sign. He is eating London's dirt, airborne essence of blackness, the last stage of the transmutation of organic detritus and minerals into dead earth. His city is the darkest recycled substance, the colour when black is burned.

Neil is stricken with an endless quest for sexual novelty. His responses to women tonight are ferociously intense: his skin prickles as the blonde waitress leaned over him with a chrome tray of canapés, her nipples thrusting through silk like a veil of bright water, her face shining like the front cover of a style mag. Because he imagines her to be unattainable, he focuses on her. His lust flings him about like a doll. He feels the pain and witnesses himself doing so from his cool, motionless observing self.

He drops down the subway steps, catching the convex hemisphere of mirror bending the foot-tunnel so it's behind a few square inches of dirty steel. He enters that tunnel, stepping over a star of drying vomit. Tunnels are the infrastructure of the spectacular city, down to the sewers that service the towering spires of the collective dream-eternity. This one smells of urine. Before the restaurant tonight he was reviewing the TV montage he had made in the previous night's magical delirium. It is a cut-up of world-changing images, in which Neil has found his Ragnarok: In a hotel room, in front of diamond-lattice wallpaper, the eyes of Khan, the dealer in illicit nukes, gaze into the end of time.

Neil is hospitable, and often hosts the moot's out-of-town guests. Typical quote, delivered with a smile: *It's all just going down the pan anyway.*

In a very special place in everyone's heart is the venerable Stan, a refugee from another era, a time-traveler who remembers witchcraft being punishable by the law, which just happens to be his own profession. He is in tweeds and open-necked shirt, smoking a pipe. Long, thin grey hair is brushed straight back over a high forehead. He traveled the world in his youth, always as more than a mere tourist, extending the natives a natural sympathy far in excess of the minimal compassion of a gentleman. Now he exudes the same sage harmony in the psychic crossfire of the moot. Typical quote: *The Goddess is the main thing.*

And then there are the minor players such as Keith, or, as he prefers to be known, Damien. Flat grey eyes scan the moot from behind a skein of greasy black hair. He never smiles, so as not to crack his faux-teenage Satanic gloom. Typical quote: *I didn't have any money for the bus fare.*

Nor must we forget Simon, a visiting organizer from another pub moot. He has eyes like a dead fish, and a sour, downturned mouth. He has a reputation for slyness, hence his nickname, Slimy Simon. He is 43 years old and lives with his mother. Typical quote: *I don't know. I don't know.*

Let Eleanor start the action: She is statuesque, big green eyes that gaze fearlessly, walking as if she is special and exempt. She has rushed across town from her design office, was delighted with how overwhelmed she felt as she squeezed into the room. She wriggled through to the bar and ordered a vodka and Red Bull. Standing on tiptoe, scanning over the sea of heads, she made out chubby, enthusiastic Gemma in the corner. Gemma's florid face creased in a big smile, and she waved El over, shoving people's coats along to make room on the bench. Eleanor was eager to gossip. In her pocket was a silk scarf, consecrated the previous night during ferociously energetic sex, and carrying a spell to bring her friend Timothy the lover of his choice. She pushed through the throng and sat down, hugging her friend. Eleanor conceals her extreme sensitivity by training furiously. Her typical quote is on the swell of her t-shirt: *PAIN IS JUST WEAKNESS LEAVING THE BODY.*

Gemma is a big-built, voluptuous, pleasure-loving redhead with a riotous laugh. She was drinking Jack Daniels and Coke, and wearing a locket charged with menstrual perfume, to bring a particular man into her bed. Typical quote: *Get it while you can, sweetie!*

So, five spells so far: three love spells, a power spell, and some kind of a destructive working. A lively little scene. Later, I will tell of another three spells, which don't just make a difference, but make all the difference.

Let the action continue.

When Eleanor had settled in, she noticed Slimy Simon sitting across the table from her. She gave him her big, open gaze and, in turn, he grazed her face with a pallid facsimile of a smile. She kept on watching him for a moment. There was something wrong with him - the man was scratching constantly. Gemma saw the direction of El's gaze, leaned over and whispered in her ear. Apparently, Slimy had boasted at some moot that he had led a curse to "teach a lesson" to some magicians who he disapproved of. Slimy's story was repeated, and grew in the telling. People had enjoyed the frisson of black magic in the cozy warmth of pub moots, but suspected in their more sober moments that the story was spun around a kernel of untruth. In fact, Slimy had never been the same since his boast.

Gemma's voice rose as she was born up into her story. Eleanor glanced over at Slimy, who looked shifty. She asked 'Ghod, what does he do in life?'

'He's applied to be a bloody magistrate!' Gemma shrieked momentarily, with the ecstasy of revelation. Slimy turned in his seat, as if his upper half was locked, stiff. Foetid air wafted over as his jacket moved, and the two friends turned to watch the rest of the room.

Bob was having an amazing time; he felt like the eyes of every woman in the place were on him. It was going to be hard to choose, very hard, he thought. The bliss of the beer rose up in him, he swallowed and exhaled, and caught Gemma's fierce gaze. Her smile spread into a filthy grin, and he fingered the keyring as she caressed her locket, making their contract across the charged and noisy air. Eleanor picked up the last part of this exchange, then turned, smiling, to Timothy, to kiss him and press the scarf into his hand. It was all working out so well. Timothy's eyes sought out Jeanette's head of long hair, swishing as she held forth. Tears stung in his diamond-bright eyes, hope choking him into silence as Jeanette turned and smiled at him, right at him. Eleanor squeezed his hand and whispered 'Go on, ask her!'

Between that moment and the morning some new things were to happen, as you may imagine. Promises will be made, to be kept, or broken. Beds will be bounced on in new rhythms, or in old ones with new flesh. Eyes will reflect a dawn over a grey skyline that throbs with the beat of the blood. Tears, dilated pupils, cries and sighs will show that minds have left time and entered mythic eternity.

The rest of the tale unfolded over the next few weeks. Drunkenly misinterpreting something Jeanette said, Gemma plucked a long, dark hair from the hairbrush she found by the bed, when she visited Bob the second time. It had to be Jeanette's and she wasn't going to be spoken to like that. She wound it into a wax doll she sculpted that night, a doll she then really couldn't decide what to do with. She was starting to realise how addicted she was to Bob's body. Deprived of that comfort when he was away, all her passion turned sour, and she spent a sleepless night glaring at the mannequin.

Jeanette, also on her own the same night, was awed and somewhat overwhelmed by the ecstasy of Timothy's passion for her. She was working on her latest book, relieved that Bob had gone. She switched the computer off and poured a glass of white wine. She asked herself once more if she could fall in love with Timothy, the way he was in love with her. As she reached for the glass, there was a spectacular crash from the direction of the kitchen. Her heart leapt, and she wandered, dumbstruck through the house. A pile of dishes had just fallen off the draining board and shattered on the tiles. She stood in the doorway, breathing fast for a while, confused, then fetched the brush and pan and swept up the mess. She returned to her Chardonnay, to wonder and reflect on this new dimension. Was she so off centre with Timothy that she was emitting raw psychic energy? She remembered her friend Anna, who people called Anna the Poltergeist, because she was always around when people's TV sets or cars blew up; was she turning into Jeanette the Poltergeist?

She poured another glass and decided to entertain an even weirder notion: that someone else was sending the energy at her. Naaah. Psychic attack hardly ever happens, and who would be so motivated? That silly cow Gemma had Bob now, which was all she wanted from Jeanette, and she didn't think she had any other enemies. Bob himself? Although generous in nature, he did have a nasty streak she'd seen emerge a few times, especially lately. The last fortnight had been horrible; when a couple falls out of love they leave little disasters around the house for each other. They are targeted, these packages of spite, cruise missiles of the heart, because the two know each other so well. Was this something like that, something semi-conscious on Bob's part, spilling out from his subconscious?

Maybe so; or maybe it's me; or maybe it's nothing at all, she concluded. As she poured the last of the wine out, the green, bubbly glass shattered. She raised her hands to her face in a reflex of fear, wide-eyed at the wine plashing onto her polished wooden floor. She reviewed her conclusions about what was happening, and began to plan her own defensive moves.

Over the next week, Gemma's possessiveness began to alienate Bob. Turning over uneasily in her bed, he spotted a wax doll part-wrapped in a cloth, on the dressing table. 'What's that, Gem?'

By the next weekend, he was back knocking on his and Jeanette's old door, apologizing and wanting his marriage back. Jeanette was having none of it, not yet anyway, and Bob had to go and stay with Neil.

Gemma was not well-pleased with Bob's desertion, and was feeling pretty bad herself. She was sick, couldn't get out of bed. She began to suspect that Jeanette had launched something against her, and she redoubled her own focus on the doll.

The next two moots were cancelled, as the casualties mounted. Bob lost his job and stayed indoors drinking for a week. Gemma shivered with fever in her bed. Jeanette and Timothy battened down the magical hatches south of the river at Timothy's flat and stayed away from the scene.

That was all last Autumn. And how did it all end? Because it did end.

As the conflicts unfolded, sweet, sensitive Eleanor had got really fed up with it. *We argue ceaselessly*, she thought, *when we are not patting each other on the back. In the moot, we huddle together, like animals warm in a communal burrow, the ritual of the booze cementing our easy chatter, knowing that life is a rage of friction and death a freezing emptiness.*

In her sadness she did a little spell to put a stop to the bitchcraft.

A stop: You know how each enchantment is a force looking for a weak point; it finds the weak point, and pushes, or pulls, and something comes apart. This final spell, to put an end to all of the conflict, found that the easiest way to do so was to end a life.

The road was slippery, and Stan was driving back from a Lodge meeting in Southampton, the yellow lights of the A34 slick on black ice. He had drunk far more than the legal limit at the festive board, toasting old friends in ruby wine, careless of his rich and love-filled life. He was flying along and didn't slow in time for the patch of fog, stamping the brake too hard for the slick surface. The car started to spin, and everything slowed down as the offside bumper caught the central barrier. Somehow the billiard-ball laws of chance flung the car over and over, crushing the nearside front corner of the old Vauxhall against Stan's skull. The surgical intervention came too late, and he was weak from the loss of blood. He never recovered consciousness.

In the peacemaking aftermath of Stan's death, Eleanor blamed herself for it. Maybe she could have chosen not to; who can say that sorcery is ever proven? We boast of the good results and choose to ignore the bad ones.

As for me, how come I can tell so much about these people? Like I said earlier, I know them. I know them because I taught them a bit of real sorcery. And because I slept with four of them, and a fifth stood by.

Of course, they came back together. There was anger and hurt between them, but the need for each other was greater. Also predictably, they scapegoated me, but couldn't drive me away, because they weren't strong enough.

And because I provide the vital spark that ignites the story-making of the City, the story-making that their fragile immortality is predicated on. To be even a little bit immortal without feeding the City, you need to be very strong.

I left anyway. Eleanor came to stay with me. That lasted a week.

Oh, I almost forgot Slimy Simon. You probably heard that little bit of scandal about him. Well, someone had to make it known. Judge me, if you will.

Specialist healing Dwarf

Chapter 9
Ragnarok

In the Voluspá, or Seeress's Prophecy of the Elder Edda we find these dramatic phrases:-

The sun turned dark, and the land sank into the sea
The bright stars fell from heaven.
Steam and fire ferment.
Flames leap high to heaven itself. [1]

Our ancestors told tales of gods ensnaring themselves in webs of *orlog*, of the ancient layers of cause and effect. They were powerfully aware of the consequences of their actions, and saw that it would be likewise for their gods.

At some stage, the drive to destruction and transformation becomes inevitable and imminent. The volva who dictated *Völuspá* had such a vision of the inevitable: she tells of the Ragnarok. The word means something like 'fate or doom of the gods'.

Ragnarok is the point where the conflicts implied by the corruption of the previous cycle of time break out into the open and are resolved. Effectively, the forces that split and differentiated at the beginning of the cycle recombine violently and annihilate each other. So that Thor meets his enemy, the world-serpent Jormungand, and they destroy each other. Odin meets Fenrir, the wolf-creature that has been chained thanks to Tyr 's sacrifice early in the history of the Aesir.

These wild, thurs-like forces, primal pre-conscious entities, meet their Aesiric equivalents, the Aesir being the guardians and guarantors of the enclave of intelligence and relative peace which is Asgard. Odin forever schemes to acquire knowledge to avoid in some way the effects of

108

Ragnarok, as we all strive to hang on to what we value, what we are responsible for. But Odin's very existence, and his will to generate intelligence in the world, exacts a price in him; in a certain sense, the Fenriswolf is the dark shadow of Odin. Perhaps more precisely, Loki is that very being – Odin's shadow – wild irresponsible intelligence that pushes evolution ahead by its destruction of forms. Loki simply must be chained for any kind of social order to evolve – but he is always there under the earth, the madman in the cellar.

Also, the world tree Yggdrasil is renewed in the course of the Ragnarok. This was necessary as the tree is eroded, tired out, by continual attrition: four harts nibble its highest boughs, serpents gnaw its branches, and the dragon Nidhogg gnaws at its roots. The nightmares of the culture, the compromises of its history, sap its vitality and newness.

Ultimately, renewal is promised, a new Golden Age. Everything is miraculously restored, washed clean by the dark transformation. The Aesir meet on Idavollr, glossed by Simek[2] as 'continually renewing, rejuvenating field':

The Aesir meet in Ida-Vale
and talk of the mighty Midgard worm,
recalling the mighty doom
and Fimbulty's ancient runes.
They will again find the wondrous
gold chess pieces in the grass,
those they had owned in the days of yore.

And there is yet a reminder that this is not the final
end, but the start of another cycle:
The dark drake comes flying,
the flashing viper from under Nitha-Fells
She sees Nithogg carrying corpses in his feathers
as he flies over the valley. Now she shall sink down.

So what does Ragnarok mean for us? Ragnarok exists on every level of reality. One obvious meaning is in the great cycles of planetary time.

Great cycles, ice-ages and the end of empires

Much can be said about the great cycles of earth and space. We prefer to imagine that things are basically quite stable on the surface of this planet, but increasingly, there is evidence that this is far from the case: that Gaia gets out more than we think, that our planet has relationships with neighbouring lumps of rock and ice. We can identify Surt the fire-giant as a comet, one of those harbingers of ill luck, who strikes and burns the earth, tilts the axis and causes the Fimbulwinter, and the ice sheets' re-encroachment. Survivors amongst the Northern peoples all around the globe have to migrate south, into the new coastal regions opened up by the expansion of the ice-caps and the concomitant drop in sea-levels. They retain a memory of the previous Northern civilization as they move southwards. This is the Thule cycle of myths, relating to the beginnings of glaciation.

Then at the other end of the cycle comes the bleeding of Ymir, the floods that deluge the world. Coastal settlements are abandoned and people have to migrate north again. This is the Atlantis cycle of myths – islands are swamped by rising waters or sink under the waves. This is a myth whose time has come again.

Another cycle of urgent relevance today is of the crises in societies and cultures. There are many reasons to believe that this civilization is approaching an end, and many people long for something better.

Would it not be the best of all worlds to live in a society where we preserve the best features of all the societies we know about? But the laws and ethics of a society depend on what is happening in the wider world of that society. We owe the abolition of slavery to the new source of labour in machines, and the line could slip if the present society broke down in certain ways.

And what if this civilization suddenly breaks down? Will we have learned anything from it, preserved anything useful from its collapse? Can we remember, as a culture, the lessons of previous civilizations? Or can every trace of history be deleted after the Ragnarok, so that we end up in the same place as we started this cycle, grubbing around in Ái and Edda's hut?

If we do bring anything from one cycle to the next, what is it? Depending on the extent of the collapse, varying amounts of technological knowledge might be saved, to form the basis for building a technological civilization again.

Some modern developments in ethics we take for granted are likely to have a short life in the stressed communities of a post-collapse world. It seems highly unlikely that the present high valuation of human life in developed societies can (or even should) persist long when the reality of overpopulation versus plummeting resources hits us. The relativity of ethics is no longer a philosophical nicety – those who constantly turn the other cheek end up cheekless except in the most exceptionally kind circumstances.

Either voluntarily or by the forces of famine, war and pestilence, the human race has to come back into balance with available resources. Through all these changes, the magician of the North keeps one eye fixed on Thule, the esoteric location where his power comes from.

The Ragnarok also refers to our own death, and how we deal with it.

Spirits in the rock

The oldest image of the world of spirits and the dead may be that they exist behind the membrane of a rock face. So that in *Hyndluljóð* we read:

...now all that rock has turned to glass;/ he reddened
it anew/ with blood of oxen;...

By smearing a rock cairn with sacrificial blood it is rendered transparent, a window into the spirit realm inside the rocks. Very ancient traditions, back to when our ancestors shared western Europe with the Neanderthals (and probably other hominid species too), tell us that the dead and the spirits live inside rocks. David Lewis-Williams[3] argues that the cave art of Lascaux is a way of entering the spirit world in trance. 15-20,000 years later, the builders of Stonehenge may well have built around the same idea. In *Hengeworld*,[4] Mike Pitts argues that the megaliths are set up for the ancestors. Northern stories abound with people entering rocks and meetings dwarves (the Brisingamen tale in *Sorla thattr*), the dead and other beings. In the Old Icelandic Rune Poem we read: 'Thurs is the torment of women, and the dweller in the rocks, and the husband of Vardh-runa'. There are hills such as Helgafell in western Iceland wherein the dead are said to exist.

There are those today who tell us that one day we will be able to upload ourselves into the mineral environment of a computer, to live another version of such an after life in a new kind of silicon tomb.[1]

The ancients also seemed to use burial mounds as sweat rooms.[5] This custom may be reflected in Gisli's Saga, where it is Thorgrim's custom to hold a festival at winter-nights in early October, where they welcomed winter and sacrificed to Freyr. After 'he had been lain in his cairn', snow wouldn't lie on it, and shoots sprouted in midwinter.

The great dead evolve, rather than resting in peace. Traditional peoples the world over have mechanisms for changing the great dead into someone of family renown, maybe a protector of the clan, then increasing until the dead person is mythic in status, a hero. The great dead are exemplars of a heroic view of life.

John Stanley Martin makes fate and the human struggle against it the central idea in his study *Ragnarok*.[6] He declares:

> in the North the gods struggle against overwhelming odds, and, although they fall in combat, their sons wreak revenge, restore primeval order, and rule in their places. Here we find the mainspring of action in an heroic society: the inner triumph of man is his struggle against irresistible forces.

Now it is a commonplace truth that we don't always get what we want – comfort, food, sex, healing, attention - and that we often get what we don't want – rejection, hunger, pain, sickness and death. This is obvious to anyone who isn't living an extremely coddled existence. Money insulates us from the worst effects of the world – bourgeois consciousness always seeks to deny the tragic dimension of life. Still, most people in the world feel that tragedy vividly because they are not sealed off from it. And anyone in an advanced industrial society who wakes up and looks around will also feel it, because it is impossible to seal ourselves off perfectly from it.

How we deal with these facts is the interesting part. The religious believer seeks to hide, alleviate, numb down the terrible idea of personal annihilation by comforting fantasies, soft lies, homilies for children. The mystic seeks to cure the terror by direct encounters with nothingness. The Buddhist way is to reject the reality of flesh-experience and practice meditation to develop equanimity towards both pleasure and pain.

In contrast, the Northern way is to extol courage. 'Courage prevails against all things' in the words of the song. The basic given here is that life may be hard, but well worth living. In *Hávamál* 76 we read:

Cattle die, kinsmen die,
and you yourself shall die.
But fair fame never dies
for the one who wins it.

It is our response to change, in the broadest sense, our transcendence of the body's reflex of fear at any change, that comprises one of the core features of illumination. Modeled on the Elder Futhark, the First Airt can be seen as our naïve, youthful nature before it is challenged by the concrete presence of death. The Second Airt is all to do with change, the development of a more conscious mental life. It starts with hagalaz: 'wreaking... havoc to the serpent': the automatic, pre-conscious life is disrupted as we grow up. Change must begin with a raising of standards, a dissatisfaction, even a trauma. Organic unity is broken into by the compassionless force of inorganic change - the hailstone. The centrality of *hagalaz* to the illuminatory process is indicated by its position as the ninth rune.

Illumination is driven by the mystery of death. The ego must reach its limits before we can begin to grow in power and awareness. Ragnarok can be seen as what happens when it's time to pay the piper, or, if you like, the opportunity to transform ourselves. For years we compromise, then the proximity of death wakes us up. The necessary corruption of compromise has eaten away at the integrity of the tree of our life. We are confronted with the *orlog*, the layers of our past actions.

What happens at this point is the collapse of a relative illusion, the moment of awakening when the dream disperses.

This is rather like the opening of the eye of Shiva, that other Indo-European god of illumination with a special eye.

Our Ragnarok is a discontinuity, an interruption in time, when eternity pours in and engulfs the mundane mind. The point of view that survives this assault of naked reality is the eye of the Hawk, the observing self sitting 'between the eyes of the eagle', always beyond and behind the immediacy of sensation and perception, beyond and behind the film show of life. That point of isolate intelligence overviews the patterns of the whole cycle from its standpoint outside of time, its eternal, hovering presence. The Hawk sees the whole Tree, Eagle-self troubled by Nidhogg-death, the nibbling attrition of daily stress, the resacralization of the flesh and of time.

The engines of change then rumble into action again, and our point of view dives into detail, embeds itself in everyday life, once more.

Of course, our animal nature wishes to forget that awful moment of naked awareness, that Ragnarok - but Odin's gift pushes us to strive to remember, to hold onto the whole picture that we saw, and to use that awareness in our Works. The ideal we clung to is broken, yet life continues; the gods are restored, and hidden in the tree of life are Life and Lifthrasir ('striving after life'). Ragnarok has renewed us, we are cleansed, we begin again, with new wisdom, having shed part of the ideal, the delusion, that was holding us in its grasp.

To the brave may come the vision of the Valkyrie.

The Valkyrie and the moment of death

Our tradition says that the warrior chosen by Odin to pass Heimdall and cross Bifrost for Valhalla will be taken up by his Valkyrie. This transport to the abode of heroes is the kind of immortality that inspires the living community we leave behind. What might this transport to Valhalla mean to the one undergoing it?

Edred Thorsson's identification of the Valkyrie with the contrasexual *fylgia*-figure, opens the possibility that the dying magician experiences a subjective eternity of rapture in the arms of his Valkyrie.[2] She, the contrasexual 'anima' figure, is in fact a perfect Other, with whom we experience the bliss of transpersonal rapture. This possibility is strengthened by the curious neurochemical observation that a flood of our very own endogenous psychedelic, dimethyltryptamine (DMT) is released into the brain at the point of death. It is one step from the extreme time-dilation typical of DMT experiences to an awe-inspiring speculation: that the point of death could become a subjective, relative-eternity in the dying minutes and hours of a consciousness well-prepared. The appearance of the perfect Other, the Valkyrie, would be a consummation devoutly to be desired, an alchemical marriage for all subjective eternity, a conscious passage from body-consciousness to an intimate consciousness of the transpersonal, the valkyrie flooding the dying brain with the final and sweetest mead, bearing the Chosen soul to the ecstasy of Valhalla or Folkvang.

The Adept at the point of death is passing into timeless rapture and yet leaving behind for his tribe the image of himself in Valhalla, as an inspiration to the living.

1. The idea that human consciousness is something that can 'run' in another 'computing environment' is based on no evidence beyond the occasionally-useful analogy between some of our mental processes and machine computation. It is not a rigorously-demonstrated fact, or even a strong hypothesis, but an article of religious faith amongst cyber-immortalists. The result of apparently 'uploading' a human consciousness may simply be a machine that behaves like a

human (i.e. it passes the famous Turing test) and claims to have subjectivity. We can, of course, never find out whether the subjectivity claimed is even of the same kind as human consciousness, let alone whether it was the subjectivity of the human who had been 'uploaded'. All we get are the claims of a bit of software that was *designed* to give the impression that it was conscious.

In my view, the extropian upload idea has enough in common with the concepts of the heavens in *Gylfaginning* to be considered a lineal descendant of them, and a source of ideas for their attempted manifestation. Not only does it call for the construction of an Andlang-like environment, out of ideas and minerals, where only non-human consciousnesses will live for the time being, but which humans will eventually live in; it also partakes of what was perhaps the same delusion that those who disappeared inside fairy hills in the old stories were suffering from in regard of the elves, the idea that humans can retain individual consciousness in that continuum. This same delusion persists in the cloud cuckoo-lands of naïve religious belief in afterlife heavens.

2. How this might apply to women in our tradition is not simple. The nature of the contrasexual Other is very different for men and women; there is no neat symmetry. However, for the purposes of this argument it is only necessary to postulate that some transcendent non-self aspect appears for either sex to be transported by.

References:

1 All Edda quotes in this chapter from the Chisholm *Edda*
2 Rudolf Simek – *Dictionary of Northern Mythology*
3 David Lewis-Williams – *The Mind in the Cave*. Thames & Hudson, 2002
4 Mike Pitts – *Hengeworld*. Arrow, 2000

5 Paul Devereux, The Long Trip, Arkana 1997.

6 John Stanley Martin – *Ragnarok: an investigation into old Norse concepts of the fate of the gods.* ISBN 90 232 1012 3

Sales and marketing Dwarf

Chapter 10
The Sky Under the Earth

'I will proceed with my history, telling the story as I go of small cities of men no less than of great. For most of those which were great once are small today; and those which used to be small were great in my own time. Knowing, therefore, that human prosperity never abides long in the same place, I shall pay attention to both alike....'

- Herodotus, introduction to *History*

The apprentice shaman found the dragon egg while he was gathering herbs, up on Ghost Hill. Nobody except the shamans came up here if they could help it, because it was a place of power. The spirits could come for you and drag you into the rocks.

The night before, the youngster had woken from dreams with the banging of the storm. He got up and stood outside his teacher's hut, shivering to the battle-din of giants ripping the sky apart. The stream he was crossing now had new rubble in it. Most of it was a dull sheep-colour, but the light made lovely patterns on the water. He rested from his climb and let his gaze fan out into the endlessly-created-and-destroyed waves downstream from each rock. He liked to gaze at moving water; he felt in his belly some wisdom about the chaos of the waves that he couldn't find words for. As his gaze spread out and relaxed, he saw below the surface, to deeper and stiller layers of reflected light. Something flashed repeatedly down there. He dropped his collecting bag on the grassy bank and waded out into the stream. Down in the strata of light, he saw a broken egg, the egg of a dragon, a giant, filled with a fire which flexed and bulged, like it was alive. A big feeling struck and rang in his chest. He bent down and tugged at the egg. It came loose, a spurt of brown slurry swirling away from its downstream edge. He staggered sideways, trying to shift the egg to the bank of the stream, a few steps away. It proved much heavier than it looked, and it got stuck straightaway. He put his hand inside it, into the cage of dancing light, and pulled hard. Something snapped, and he felt a sharp pain. He drew his hand, streaming with blood, out of the water. He was holding a light-stone, a rock made of solid light which flashed every colour in the world as he gazed at it, oblivious to his injury. The stone had impossibly straight edges, and he remembered the time he had seen the sea and the line of its horizon, straight like the strange lines of this stone, birds crying above him.

He stood there, lost in that rapture, until pain and dizziness made him splash and stagger to the bank to deal with his hand. He sat down heavily, next to his bag, and drew a long hemp fibre from the weave of the cloth. He tied it with practiced fingers around the base of his bleeding thumb. As he tightened it, the blood flow slackened and stopped. He stood up and walked a few paces until he saw the leaves he needed. He wrapped the cut in the wound-herb, singing to its spirit as he did so. He sat back down and shifted his breathing to still himself, focussing his attention on his body-egg, so that the power-that-moves could flow better. As usual when he was mending himself, he thought for a few moments about his death and, as always, prayed he would meet the shining ones. He held the position, golden light playing on his closed eyelids, until he felt the throbbing subside.

He was unsurprised to note that he had not let go of the light-stone during all of this. He had been taught how light-stones can quicken and store the power-that-moves, and this was a very special stone, straight from the egg. Yes, he knew now how light-stones were born.

Up on the ridge above the village, the old shaman stirred his brew and sang new songs over it. His people considered him mad for wanting to make the drinking-brew. They were afraid, because the inventors of the drinking-brew were overrunning their world, cutting down the holy chaos of the timeless forests and grazing too many sheep on the thin land, the land where the brew-herbs grew now. They were afraid of their old, mad shaman, and wished he would die and join the spirits.

He in turn knew that his people were in eclipse. He had seen it all, in a vision.

He said to the boy, whom he didn't think of as having earned a proper name yet: 'No-one understands our visions, least of all us. We saw the drinking-people before they came here. You must give us a new vision. The drinking-brew is good for visions. Maybe you will take it, for the healing of the people'.

The old man left the youth to sing over the brew, while he rested his leathery old body on a pile of fur blankets. He had received the boy's awed enthusiasm over the light-stone, refusing to touch it himself, because it was the boy's own power that had brought him such a fine omen. He was becoming ready for the task the old man had for him.

That midwinter they went up to the caves. They passed by the passage-barrow. A family of chieftains had celebrated every midwinter here for eighty generations, tearing open the vulval leather curtains of the hot rebirth chamber at midwinter dawn, emerging hot-skinned in spiral swirls of smoke into that icy world. Now only their bones lay beneath the ritual floor. Two winters ago, the boy, a member of that clan, had been initiated in that chamber.

This year, they would not be sealing themselves in the great chamber with the poppy smoke; they were gone now, the elders sacrificed and most of their youngsters educated in the round, timber lodges of the drinking-people. The boy was the last of the chieftain clan, the dreamy youngster whom they'd let go, into the care of the old shaman, because he seemed fey and foolish, unsuitable to lead the new ploughing teams.

The old man led the way up into the narrow gully where the caves lay. The young one carried their bundles. The slope ran up to the lip of the cave, then they had to negotiate a narrow passage between giant boulders. They emerged into an oval cavern. At his teacher's gesture, the apprentice lay the wood down on the floor and began to build a fire.

A fog of evergreen filled the cave. They sang in the smoke, and the old man took out a closed horn of the drinking-brew. He broke the beeswax seal, held up the horn, sang louder for a while, a song in praise of the drink, then drank. He passed the rest to the youth, who felt fear in his belly, for they were calling on the spirit of the dark cave, something that was countless generations older, even, than his ancient race, the barrow-builders, and held a cold terror for them. But in his heart was his own stronger determination, and in his head was a burning curiosity, as he sang and drank, and sang again.

At the back of the cave a deep passage led down into the hillside. In the light of their pig-fat torches they saw ancient drawings on the walls, the stylized beasts and animal-headed shamans of the cave-people. In the flickering light the bison and horses bulged out of the rock walls. The youth sang softly under his breath, his heart pounding with fear, as they edged along the cleft. Finally, they reached the heart of the cave-temple, the narrowest and lowest part. The old man wedged

123

himself across the narrow floor and wrapped himself in his thick blankets. The youth looked around and saw that the tunnel continued into a crawl-space at eye-level. The old man was wrapped in his own world. The boy was on his own.

He slid into the gap on his belly until his full body length was enclosed in the ancient rock. It was comfortable and seemed warmer here. With his hands he felt around until he came upon a design carved into the rock above him. He managed to turn his body over so that he was lying on his back, facing the ceiling of the crawl-space. The faint light from the torch showed him the pattern he had felt: a series of concentric swirls connected by looping lines. Just before the torch guttered out he saw for a moment the magic patterns of the oldest, oldest script.

In the darkness the brew-spirit grabbed him, a swirl of thoughts that came from the back of his head, and, seamlessly, he knew three new things. He knew that the trust he had been given, to bring back a story to save his people, would only partially succeed: he would find his story, but it was too late to save his people; the sheep-herders and their ways had come into the world, and they would prevail for many generations to come.

He was swamped with sorrow, weeping, torn with the tragedy of it, when the two further revelations hit him: he knew that the old man would die, and that something strange and hidden awaited the youth too, in their journey through the night.

In his isolation, through the ache in his guts and the grief flooding in his tears, the brew-vision was relentless. First he saw the cave-painters, hunters dressed in skins, singing words that made no sense. One of the cave-ghosts, a broad-faced girl with a bone flute, ran towards him, butted him between the eyes and darted beyond him into the cleft.

He found himself following, becoming smaller as he wriggled deeper into the crack. Now he had no idea where his body was, and the visions intensified; his own advisor-spirit, looking like a winter fox, came to him and he followed it, crawling into a corridor of even tinier tunnels, crawling into the past.

He saw the grey swell of the sea under dark and angry skies as his distant ancestors arrived in boats, just like the legends told it, fleeing the flood that had inundated their great stone-built coastal cities.

He saw the great fields of ice that covered the world before the flood. He learned that the world is indeed not flat, but like a round rock floating in a sea that has neither up nor down, like the old shaman had told him. He saw the terrible catastrophe that had caused his people's evacuation, the giant stone hurled from the other side of the sky, striking the earth and making the waters rise.

He went back further in the ancient layers; he witnessed the previous cycle of abandonment of the Northern lands as the ice returned. He saw the terrible winter, three winters in one of deathly, freezing darkness. He saw the people of a high plain digging a vast underground city in the soft tufa rock. Then once again, he saw the re-colonization of the North as the ice sheets melted, and the floods came.

Then suddenly he was struggling out into a big chamber, like the one he had come through on his way here, but now bright with sourceless light. He stood up and faced the incredible, living paintings. These pictures were a statement that their painters were human, were like him, even though they'd dressed in skins and hunted bison on a treeless tundra. They were not trolls, the thick-browed creatures of his people's legends - he'd never seen one, but his grandfather claimed to have. No, these people had pictures in their minds, and they manipulated them to make people think of other things, just like shamans did.

And now these clever hunters were gone, left behind, forgotten in tales of the generations of people. Just like his people would disappear, be forgotten in the world of the sheep-herders. Who in turn would yield to a new race and be themselves forgotten.

He closed his eyes. His mind turned away from the past and took flight into the future. He saw vast migrations of tribes, whole peoples on the march. He saw terrible wars. He saw a great civilization spreading across the globe, building incomprehensible cities.

In his flying eye vision he picked out people of the future. He saw men and women in times to come who worship no gods or spirits, who believe only in their own power. He was drawn to these; they are outcasts like himself, exceptional outsiders who live their whole lives in exile. No family to uphold them and bury them in the sacred mound when they die. Nothing for them after death – no memory of their fame in the mind of their tribe.

Looking at the lives of these future people, he realised that he was not of his own age, but an exile in time. He opened his eyes, and standing facing the spirit-bison, he asked: if my destiny is not that of my dying race, then what is it?

For the first time then, he saw how the rock face had been rendered soft and permeable by the images painted on it. The surface of the rock was a thin, lighted membrane between his eyes and the spirit world within the rock.

He reached into his tunic and brought out the light-stone. He saw its spirit, alive with molten light, and thought of what his teacher told him: that it would act to let him into the spirit-world inside the rocks, and that he would know what to do when the time came. He saw the narrow cleft beneath the eye of the bison, and pushed the stone in.

As he gazed, the bison struggled out of the rock, its hot, beast breath in his face, its smell filling the cavern. The glow disappeared, so that he was back in darkness for a moment, then something popped in his head, and suddenly he was on the surface of the earth, under a blinding night sky bursting with fat stars, and he was not alone. A sleek-faced, bald woman had her jewelled, tattooed arms round his neck. They were entwined in sex, in the centre of a circle of singing people.

Except for her bizarre adornments, the girl looked amazingly like him, had the same colour skin and eyes, a distant granddaughter of his folk, from who-knows-how-many generations in the future. She had a muscular, well-fed body, glorious big breasts, a blade of moonlight hanging between them on a leather thong. She repeated the same words again and again, just like the old man had taught him how to call spirits. Across a gulf of uncounted years, he heard the words of her call, in a voice shrill and exultant with orgasm, *Elf, my Elf, come, my Elf...*

With a shock it hit him that it was he whom she was calling, and that he may well be dead, and lost in the spirit-world. The shock passed quickly, to be replaced by wonder, and curiosity about where his journey would take him next.

The girl released him from her clasp and he followed her gaze, up into the night sky. A rippling column of light, like a sunbeam through a hole in the clouds, gusted by winds of another world, struck the earth around them. The voice of the winds roared wordless in his head, and he looked up, and up, ...and up... to the star that formed the head of a Shining One, an elf.

The elf's towering cloak of light shimmered with tiny shapes, blown about in its rippling, a patchwork of tiny, dead human faces. He thought he saw his grandfather, the sacrificed chieftain. He opened his mouth to speak, but the cloak of dead faces rippled and the scene changed. Where the faces

127

had been were now little spinning wheels of bright fantastic colours, like the hues of a rainbow, but made of solid light. The tiny light wheels spun and sang and radiated their incredible unnatural colours.

He realised he was witnessing the next stage of the evolution of the dead. That which happens when no-one remembers any more the particular details of our lives. The memory of us is worn smooth like pebbles in the river of memory. *We lose our own faces.* Then we are ready to become these spinning wheels of colour that make up parts of the body of an elf, an elf whose body reaches to the distant stars.

He gazed up at the glory that was the elf, and knew without any doubt that this was the best death he could achieve. He opened his heart to the transformation and the sky rang, a sound like starlight fizzing in his bones. The world he had just found, he left behind again.

Lifted beyond wonder now, he sang his final song, each word taking a piece of the mind that sang it and spinning away, bright gems of solid light that sang his song forever. As he lost outline, his being joined a greater throng, and he was swept up, like a leaf in a twisting wind, and whirled into the sky under the earth, into a torrent of borderless sentience, not an I in sight, into a racing motion with a heart of pure stillness.

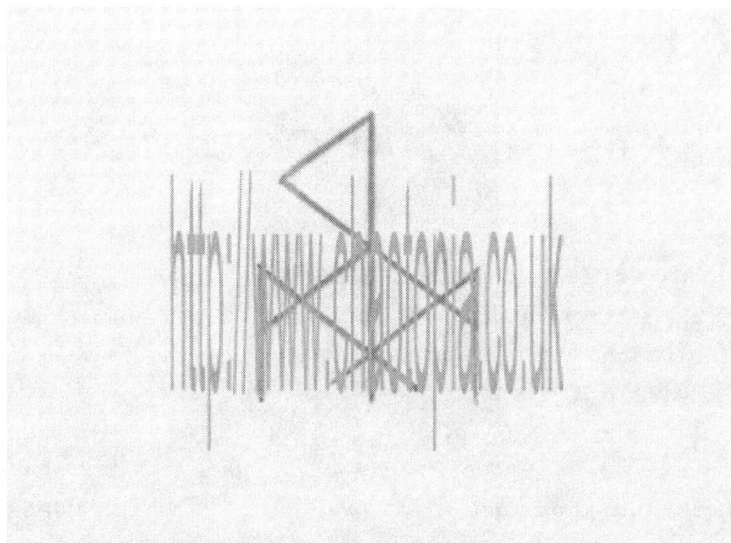

Website Dwarf

Chapter 11
Tools of Consciousness

Transcendence and Ecstasy

What are the qualities of the state we call gnosis, the extraordinary state of consciousness we use to do magic? Looking over anecdotes from Chapter 7:

In anecdote 1 a god I didn't realize was a possessing type god, possessed me so smoothly I didn't realize I had been under until it left. I was aware of something separating itself from me and saying 'bye. This was a possession trance.

In anecdote 12, where my girlfriend levitated, I thought I was in normal consciousness, but I had just finished concentrating hard and was mentally empty and relaxed. In any case, I'm by no means certain what influence my presence or state of consciousness contributed to the event.

In most of the other examples I was in a highly focused trance. I was also concentrating on externals, to the extent of holding the group working together, or of staying flexible for some reason or other.

The features that jump out are trance and flexibility of attention. So what is trance?

Perhaps the most sophisticated treatment is by A. J. Deikman, in *The Observing Self*. The observing self is what we call the experience, which occurs at a certain stage in personal development, when you become aware of yourself watching yourself. Deikman speaks of this experience as a 'transcendent' faculty in the midst of ordinary consciousness[1]. When we are aware that we are observing ourselves, then we are in a state of relative transcendence to those states. I suspect this is what Austin Spare meant by the Kia, when he describes it as the 'atmospheric I'.

The observing self forms the negative basis of Deikman's definition – he neatly opposes the observing self to the state we are mostly in, what he refers to as trance. He writes: 'trance can be understood as a loss of context'.[2]

Trance is a powerful but restricted state. Many hypnosis researchers say that all learning takes place in trance.

On the other hand, the observing self is totally flexible – it is the fluidity underlying the sense of self, and is unaffected by everything that happens. It is the source of the ability to transcend all and any trances, any restricted context whatever. It is the 'spirit of the valley' in Taoism – entirely passive, having no power at all, and yet all power. These two functions – the embeddedness of trance and the lightness of the observer self – form a spectrum that all ordinary consciousness exists on. So, when we are totally focused on our computer screen or our negative fantasy we have lost the context of our thinking, it has shrunk to the immediate content of our thoughts.

Now to be more precise as to the nature of the observing self, it doesn't really sit on a spectrum with trances at the other end. That is simply a way of thinking about it that picks out its main feature – that it is anything but a trance state. In reality, this awareness can be present at any time, and awareness of it can be cultivated by meditation. If the 'opposite' of trance is the transcendent quality of the observing self, then immunity to trance would eventually be conferred by a massively stable access to observer awareness. This appears to be what a lot of meditators are seeking – an equanimity which can pass unscathed through mob violence, addictions, death and even reality TV. Repeated access to the observing self installs that observing perspective as a habitual state of the nervous system.

The mechanism of identification is tied very closely to the state of attention, whether it is entranced or self-aware. Parsing this automatic process of identity-formation:

Whatever you are thinking or feeling, you may be aware of yourself doing so, at least from time to time. When you are intensely engaged in, for instance, a train of thoughts, you don't generally look at that activity in context; you're not aware of yourself thinking. Your sense of self is engulfed, submerged in your focused mental activity.

When you do become aware of yourself thinking, you suddenly switch to viewing yourself thinking as an object, something your subjectivity observes. Your subjectivity is no longer submerged in activity, but standing elsewhere, viewing the activity. You are in a condition of standing-apart, standing-outside, which is the meaning of the Greek word *ecstasis*. Ecstasis in this sense is the opposite of trance, identical to what Deikman calls 'transcendence'.

The mystic is a specialist in the observing self, and it seems that the higher levels of mysticism are reached by abiding in that observer position until it somehow becomes identified with everything. All trance is avoided in the mystical path, all awareness is pushed towards transcendence, towards union with the biggest contexts of all.

In contrast, the magician requires the trance-inducing intensity of passion and will to power his enchantment. And what is will? In its primal form, it is basic goal-directed activity. It is the functional mode of the object selves. Each mundane self has its own will-fragments – sex, money, security, and so on. The magical Will is the functional mode of the magical self. It is goal-directed, like the mundane, fragmented wills, but it is much more focused, and thereby more powerful than them.

Much magic is indeed done in a deep trance of belief, in a state where all context is deliberately lost, and a narrow, focused beam of fanatical obsession is achieved for the duration of the working. Such a working, at the more extreme end, may leave few traces of memory in the magician. Working with possessing spirits and gods can be like this.

However, magic can and is also done in full, conscious awareness of both the immediate and the overall context of the spell. The observing perspective is not sacrificed, and full memory of the working retained. This kind of magic is singled out for special attention by some writers. Michael Aquino, founder of the Temple of Set, refers to it as Greater Black Magic, and Edred Thorsson defines the ancient magic known as *galdor* in these terms.

Magical action of this kind depends on the observing self being so well-established that it is possible to split your attention, so that the observing self is watching the object-mind, the will, doing its magic on the world. There is then a triangle, Observer, Will and World, paradoxically superimposed.

That's how come yogis are warned of the dangers of *siddhis*, the magical powers that arise on the mystical path – they are specialists in the observing self, and their ability to do galdor-type magic is thereby strengthened over the years. They are told to reject these temptations, in order to specialize in the entirely internal work of the observer self, what is usually called mysticism. Of course, these temptations on the path are exactly what interest us as magicians.

The image of the tree of Yggdrasil seems to contain a model in mythic form of the levels of consciousness involved in magical action.

The tree is the world, and upon it depend many beings. In *Grimnismal* of the Elder Edda, (v.32) we read:

An eagle sitteth on Yggdrasil's limbs, whose keen eyes widely ken; 'twixt his eyes a fallow falcon is perched, called Vedhrfölnir, and watcheth.

The eagle is the magical self, because it is one of the beast-vehicles of magician-god Odin. One of Odin's *heiti* is Arnhofdhi, 'eagle-headed'. The falcon or hawk is the animal self of both major goddesses, Freya and Frigg, referring to their visionary powers. Further, Hollander in his translation of the Edda, comments that 'The eagle and the falcon possibly symbolize the watchfulness of the gods'. It seems to me that the hawk that sits between the eagle's eyes is the observing self.

Both these creatures sit upon the Tree, which is the World. Around its roots coil the dragon Nidhogg. These four beings – Eagle, Hawk, Dragon and Tree – give us a complete mythic representation of the galdor-magical process.

In galdor-type magic, the self is fully-conscious at the moment of projection of the will. In other words, the magical self extends its will at the same time that the observing self sees it all happen. The observing self is unfazed by the focus of the magical self – context is not lost, even though the magical self is in a narrow, focused, fanatical state. This is the nature of this kind of magic – that the observing self is present throughout it, and that the consciousness of the wizard is doubled.

So, what we are really developing in our magical work is the ability to split our attention in this way, to bring the observer-perspective into even our most passionate and intense trances. The path of the magician emphasises both the transcendent and the immanent, worldly aspects of life, in contrast to the way of the mystic, who seeks to transcend the whole show.

There is more detail yet: the magical self, the eagle, is in truth the dragon-eagle of the aroused serpent-force, the Norse equivalent of the goddess Kundalini in Hindu sexual alchemy. The dragon is the force of life and death, coiled half-asleep at the base of the spine. Because it is a giver of life and death, those two things are closely tied together in us, and often closeness to death makes us feel intensely alive. It is the dragon-force that is the source of the feeling of being alive. The dragon mutters of death and renewal, forever, without any boundaries of individual consciousness to limit its immortality in the half-light of the abyss. It lives in the moment of attention, which is then erased and replaced as its head turns. Nobel-laureate neuroscientist Gerald Edelman depicts[3] animal consciousness as a single, amnesiac torch beam, illuminating one spot at a time.

This animal half-consciousness raised to full consciousness by the Hawk's Eye of self-awareness becomes the mighty Eagle. The Dragon raised to ecstasy, in its fully-awakened form is the Eagle-Giant, the sensation of the life-force raging through us while fully conscious. The Eagle is a Giant – a pre-human, pre-Asgard force, the beating of whose wings sends out the pulse of consciousness which is the shaping force of galdor, a rhythmic wind that sweeps all before it through the nine worlds.

In the eye of this storm, between the Eagle's eyes, sits the starry-eyed Hawk. Vedhrfölnir is the Ek, the source of selfhood. The Falcon of the Ek clings to the Eagle, astride the arisen and awoken Serpent. Vedhrfölnir is the *storm-bleached*, the vanishing perspective point at the core of the mind, empty of qualities, witnessing without choice: the observing self, bleached out and shrunken to a diamond-bright point in the windstorm.

The awakened serpent-power is the magical fuel, the felt passion which drives the enchantment. The dragon-force as

Nidhogg bearing naked corpses linked to the eagle-giant Hraesvelg, 'corpse-gulper' refers to the way that awareness of the body is swallowed up in the ecstasy of the risen dragon-eagle force. This dynamic tension of opposites – the transcendent and the life-embracing – generates a circuit of higher and lower consciousness in which they both exceed their normal limits. It is this magical super-consciousness that the magician seeks to develop.

The work of magic requires transcendence, but transcendence is not its aim. The overall aim of the magical path, if I define it in a way which opposes it to the mystical path, is always to return to Midgard, with the rewards of one's magical action there for one and, if it be your Will, for all the world to see. Magic has to be a celebration of the world, of spirit in its manifest form as the flesh, the body. The magician plays with the transcendent, but always returns to the flesh. The flesh is corruptible, mortal, subject to the worst the world has to offer, but surely it is still the most precious thing, to be born into this death-bounded ecstasy.

The Work Of The Magical Self

Each of our mundane selves, the knots of desire and will that our behaviour orbits around, is an access-point to a world of its own. Each of these tunnels contains powers and is ruled by limitations. The self that negotiates these various realities I call the magical self. I prefer this term to 'Higher Self', because the latter term generally connotes a Being that pre-exists the birth of the individual self, a position I don't usually subscribe to.

The magical self has these qualities coexisting:

1. continual self-awareness; ie, the presence of the observing self, which saves the magical self from context-blindness;

2. objectivity about subjective states or the status of the other selves; the other selves are aspects of what Deikman calls the object-self, that which acts in the world.

3. Luck follows on from magical work, from magical selfhood. *Hamingja* – luck or magical power – is strengthened. More often, you feel 'in the zone'.

And:

4. This special and paradoxical self is then realised as the most perfect avatar, the most perfect self for the expression of the magician's life-force, the magician's genetic complement, and also the magician's family spirit or fylgia, whose powers run in your genes.

From the living experience of magical Selfhood, the magician can rebuild his self-complex. One way to do this is, over a series of magical retirements – concentrated sequences of daily magical work lasting a few weeks – to create your own system of magic, your personal grimoire.

In my case, I worked up from the lower levels, from a simpler level than selves. I started by constructing a set of servitors, using miniature sigil-paintings inside squares, for various faculties and skills. Examples of the types of function are included in this book.

These contain mundane considerations, and on one level can be thought of as a bit like psychological strategies – sets of instructions to the subconscious mind. However, made as they are in a magical context, they are more than that, and contain magical instructions too. If I need assistance from outside of my skin, or to influence magically the external world, that is implicit in all of them.

With these squares, I began to unfold the components of what I wanted to become, the skills and capabilities that I wanted to be part of me. I began to rebuild myself in a more organized fashion than I'd done before in previous metamorphoses. I began to complete work that I had started years before.

I came to think of these square cards as dwarves: they represent a functional kind of spirit, corresponding to personal skills or powers which make things happen in the different areas of my life. They have less depth and complexity than selves, and are essentially impersonal, which is how I can publish most of their details without causing problems for myself – they are not keys to my identity. You could take any of those glyphs, rename it for your contact with it, and use it if you wanted to.

The next stage was to create a card for a spirit that harmonized all the complex elements I'd created. At first, I had only that idea – something to harmonize it all. But in considering the position an entity would have to be in, in relation to the smaller spirits in order to do the harmonizing, I could see that this would have to be a bigger, more complex and flexible spirit. In fact, it was more or less by definition my magical self. This was an octagonal form.

This level is deeper and more inclusive – higher, if you like – than the servitor-spirits of the square cards. It's also higher level, deeper and more complex, than a self. How? By the fact that it contains at its core the self-making faculty, the faculty of identifying with some entity, some spirit, some structure, and thereby making it yourself. This I symbolized by the Valknut.

Now there is a third level, which lies in between the squares and the octagon. I defined the hexagon as the realm of the mundane selves. Right from the start, it became clear to me that our normal, mundane selves are best characterized as demons. Any structure at the level of the functional selves, the repositories of our identities on a day to day basis, is bound to be demonic, in the sense of limited and limiting.

Why?

Identification with a mundane self occurs when the observing faculty is not noticed any more. When we are in trance, in a limited frame of reference, our identity is submerged in the will of the object-self we are identified with.

Ultimately, the selves are illusory because their 'contents' – i.e. the processing the self causes – are limited and limiting, cyclical processes that generate a protected, locked state. They consist, if you like, of the walls around specific trances, if we define trances as the loss of conscious context, a narrowing of consciousness.

In contrast, the observing self cannot be an object, because it is what objectifies the other, object selves. It is at the centre of the identity, the Hawk sitting between the eyes of the Eagle of the magical self.

The mundane selves are illusions of self-hood suited to objectified commerce with the world. The object selves can be seen as contracted selves, because they have contracted frames of reference, contracted senses of context.

That's how come they have outlines and can be seen as objects, can be studied by mundane psychology, because they are not fully conscious – although they'd have you think they are. They are limited cycles of predictable behaviour. They run us most of the time, when we are on automatic, when we are asleep in the Gurdjieffian sense.

They are trapped in a cycle of self-referentiality, of repetitious claiming of the energies of the host-body, taking those energies and spewing out the particular pattern of emotional and mental states we come to associate with that demon, with that self. These ordinary selves are illusory. They are entirely Choronzonic, in the chaos-magical sense of being based on misidentifications.

They are the mutterings of Nidhogg the dragon at the base of the Tree, at the base of the spine, as it stirs in its heavy, reptilian half-sleep, its one eye heavy-lidded.

These mutterings are taken up by Ratatosk, the squirrel that is the internal monologue. The squirrel parlays the innocent venom of the dragon into frissons of death-anxiety and of ego-rebellion against the end of selfhood. With these thoughts it troubles the Eagle, the Self that raises itself above the tumult. The Hawk's attention and thereby its perspective is lost as the Will is fragmented by the concerns of the object-selves.

It is possible to negotiate with the selves, with your demons[4]. In the process of negotiating with them, you will discover that the self that is doing the communicating is the point of attention around which you are building your magical self. The perspective from which you communicate with the selves is the magical self. You will note the sense of additional degrees of freedom, of power.

This realization, this concrete awareness of the illusoriness of the mundane selves encourages the return, again and again, to transcendent states – magical work refreshes the taste of true Selfhood, and passive meditation refreshes the Will, by giving it a rest.

This becomes the motivation in itself to continue with our magical work. This, and the observation that something in us – i.e. the magical self – gets stronger, and so our luck improves, our ability to flow through the world and do our will improves.

'A word led to a word
A work led to another work'

- Hávamál

The Triple Gift

Odin, Vili and Ve, or in another version of the tale, Odin, Hoenir and Lothur give the three gifts to mankind, ensouling us with three attributes:

140

From the host came three,
mighty and powerful Aesir, to coast.
There they found an ash and an elm
of little might, and lacking orlog.
They had neither breath nor wit nor life hue
nor manner nor good looks. Odin gave them
the breath of life, Hoenir gave them wod,
Lothur gave them life and good looks.

The gift of Lothur, *lau* – blood, heat of life, looks, seems
to refer to the human face, the individual and the legacy of
the family line observable in the face. The work associated
with this level would be bodywork and the maintenance and
balancing of the mundane selves.

The gift of Odin, *önd*, refers to breath. This aspect of
life is non-individual, drives and moves the body without
consciousness. It is, however, very close to consciousness;
breath is one of the few automatic functions that
consciousness can intervene in directly, and anyone who has
practised conscious breathwork can attest the power of breath
to affect your conscious state.[5] Connected breathwork is a
particularly accessible form of meditation, in the sense of
developing reflexive self-awareness, as well as conferring
mundane benefits.

The gift of Hoenir, is of consciousness itself – wod,
odhr – ecstasy and inspiration. Hoenir, giver of ecstasy, is one
of the survivors of Ragnarok into the new cycle. The
transcendent faculty, the Eye of the Hawk, flies over the
tumult of life's endings and beginnings, forever observing
without intervening.

Let us look at other possibilities opened up by a law of
threes in your being: base, heart and head.

The base is the realm of the dragon, the instincts, the
reptile-brain. It is pre-personal and immortal. It is fed by

pleasure, ecstasy and danger, anything that makes you feel more alive. It doesn't care if you live or die, as long as it's intense. It simply moves on to another body. You can keep it manifesting through your particular body by a combination of luck (i.e. magical power) and attendance to good health.

The centre realm is the heart, the trunk of the tree, the personal, emotional self, the mammal-brain. This suffers daily attrition from the harts of stress, and the anxious wittering and delusions of the squirrel-mind. It is preserved by the application of the sacred white clay and water, which is to say it is fed by simplicity and discipline. It is also fed by social satisfaction, both bonding and status, and social games.

The upper realm is that of the Eagle and Hawk. This is everything from the verbal faculty up to superconsciousness and the transpersonal. The Eagle is fed by magic and by ecstasy and awe, the Hawk by meditation and lucid dreaming. The Eye of the Hawk is strengthened by any work of self-observation. The Hawk and the Eagle are both strengthened immeasurably by regular magical work, developing the doubling of attention during magical action.

A Ritual

What follows is a ritual to raise the Dragon-Eagle energy into full consciousness. The ritual can be used as a preliminary to galdor, or as a daily exercise to raise power.

This form of the working is just one example. Once the principle is grasped, the working can be adapted into other forms. You could use different galdors or other techniques altogether, drawn from the disciplines of magic, meditation and body-energy work to fill the basic steps 1-5.

The Hawk is invoked, then the Dragon, then they are combined, and the Inner Mead is made. As mentioned in Chapter 2, the mead of inspiration, Odhroerir, is made of the blood of the wise Kvasir, a being formed from the combined spittle of the Aesir and the Vanir and so carrying the wisdom of both races of gods. Two principles – the earthy wisdom of the Vanir and the celestial consciousness of the Aesir are wedded to form a third mighty power. In the circulation of energy outlined below, the two principles of bodily dragon-energy and Hawk-consciousness are combined to form a third, the Inner Mead, through the medium of spittle.

This form of the working relies on the practice of circulating body energy around the torso. When you first start doing this, the impression is that you are circulating your attention. With practice, the sensation changes to that of energy entrained by the circulation of attention so that it follows the motion. The practise of visualizing energy circulating up and down around the body develops the observing capacity, the passive, detached perspective. This can be located in a space inside the head.

The first stage is to circulate the energy from the base centre, around the perineum, up the back of the torso on the inhale, through the gate of the throat as the inhale changes to exhale, down the front of the torso with the exhale and through the gates of the perineum wth the change to inhale.

When you are practised at this visualization, speed it up, so that the circulation goes much faster than the breath. You don't have to keep the circulation going really fast – the point is to decouple it from the breath rhythm for a while to open up your awareness of what you are doing. You begin to be aware of the observer that is observing all this, the point of attention with which you are aware of the circulation. This is the basis of the next stage.

Cultivate awareness of a point in the head, typically a few inches back from the brow, from which you observe the movements of energy. This is the Seat of the Hawk. Cultivate a dual awareness, of the energy circulation through the torso and the bright point of attention in the head. Now you are ready to practise the final stage of the ritual, the making of the Inner Mead.

The working has been done in groups using breathwork for the Work of the Hawk and movement for the Work of the Dragon. Some remarkable effects have been created, such as a large proportion of the group seeing auras.

Another extension to this working is into sexual alchemy. The rising dragon-force of sexual excitement is suspended from release and circulated, the downward gaze of the Hawk meeting it in the roof of the mouth to generate the risen dragon-eagle state of ecstasy, when an extraordinarily potent Inner Mead can be formed.

The whole working can be regarded as a triple working of evocation, consciousness-raising and invocation. Following this idea, you could invoke a deity into the inner mead and then into yourself.

Another way of looking at this working is as a wheel or cycle of alchemical principles, the stages of alchemical substance. The Dragon refers to Salt in Western alchemy, or *tamas* in the Hindu gunas, the Hawk to Mercury or *sattvas*, the Eagle to Sulphur or *rajas*. The entire working then becomes a meditation on how one kind of energy or stage of conscious experience changes into another.

Stage 1

Honour the Dragon, the Hawk and the Eagle, for example with the galdor **ULS(e)HAI.**

(The (e) represents the neutral vowel sound of 'e' in the English word 'the'.)

Stage 2, the Work of the Hawk

This is the phase of cultivating conscious awareness. For this stage use any discipline which cultivates the sense of observing yourself, such as breathwork[6] or self-observing forms of meditation. You can also use the following galdor.

However, don't use the galdor until you have a state to link it to, until you have formed a clear sense of self-observation through one or other meditative practice. Then the galdor becomes a link to that state. It is formed from ᚺ *hagalaz*, the centre of the ice-crystal, ᛁ *isa*, the point of attention and ᚨ *ansuz*, consciousness, forming the idea of a consciousness-ice-crystal: **HAI.**

Stage 3, the Work of the Dragon

This is the evocation phase, in which you are working with physical and emotional energy. Stand and shake, let the power get loose, shake and shiver. If you are working out of doors, let the cold come inside you and shiver with the power. Stamp your feet, feel the solidity of the earth as power, rising through you, the life-in-death of the dragon-seed or dragon-egg in your belly, feel the wetness and heat of your flesh. This phase of the working could consist of dancing to music with a driving rhythm.

Feel the Dragon force through your sexuality, through your fear, through your love, your greed, your anger, everything and anything that gets you worked up.

Circulate the forcer round and round your body. The consciousness of the Hawk doesn't interfere, and the Dragon doesn't even discriminate. All that matters is intensity. When you feel a desire to move, go along with it. To shake, to crawl, to form your body into the way it wants to go, follow only the dictates of the pleasure-energy in you, your guide to the life-death force of the Dragon.

Use the galdor for the Dragon: From ᚢ *uruz*, primal life force, wild beast, and *laguz*, water-serpent, the rune ᛚ an upright form of the serpent that encircles the earth, Jormungandr: **UL.**

Stage 4, arousal of the Dragon-Eagle

This is the invocation stage. From the vantage point of the Hawk, circulate the power around the body. Start with bringing it up your back as you breathe in, down your front. Split your attention so that you are simultaneously aware of the bright, wind-bleached realm in the head, and the surging power of the body-energy.

There is a gap you are going to close between the earth and the sky perspectives, in the roof of your mouth.

Use the Eagle galdor, from ᛋ *sowilo*, the raging force of the sun, and the column, ᛇ *ihwaz*: **S(e).**

Stage 5, the making of the Inner Mead

Feel the dual principles simultaneously, feel them creating a third being. Feel this being loaded with wisdom, with power, with whatever type of force you need.

Sing the galdor of the risen dragon-eagle – **ULSEHAI.**

Feel the power of the risen dragon meeting the gaze of the Hawk. Feel the streams of force blending to form a third – the Mead.

Make the Mead in your mouth. Let the energy of it build up for a few more cycles of circulation, then swallow it.

Feel the power coursing through you, going to where you directed it.

Notes

1. Quote: Deikman, p95
   'The observing self is not part of the object world formed by our thoughts and sensory perception because, literally, it has no limits; everything else does. Thus, everyday consciousness contains a transcendent element that we seldom notice because that element is the very ground of our experience. The word *transcendent* is justified because if subjective consciousness - the observing self - cannot itself be observed but remains forever apart from the contents of consciousness, it is likely to be of a different order from everything else. Its fundamentally different nature becomes evident when we realise that the observing self is featureless; it cannot be affected by the world any more than a mirror can be affected by the images it reflects.'

2. The full quote is:
   'trance can be understood as a loss of context. Most of the time we function within a conceptual framework of which we are only marginally aware, a context that places us in time, geographic area, culture and social role and provides self-definition. .... my activity is given meaning and direction by a loose backdrop of concepts and memories that place me in the flow of experience. ... in hypnosis the frame of reference is 'contracted'.'

3. Gerald Edelman – *Bright Air, Brilliant Fire: On the Matter of the Mind.* Penguin, 1994.

4. I recommend *Uncle Ramsay's Little Book of Demons* by Ramsey Dukes for powerful models of how to negotiate with them.

5. Ingrid Fischer (RuneGild communication, 2005) notes the connection of *önd* with the kidneys. An energy associated with breath– *chi* – is also considered in Chinese alchemy to be stored particularly in the kidneys.

6. For information on breathwork, visit my website at www.chaotopia.co.uk

References
A J Deikman – *The Observing Self*

Chapter 12
Rune - Poem

ᚠ

1. FEE to be free must freely be given;
gold hoarded makes human cattle;
the serpent's shining scales crawl with fatal envy.

ᚢ

2. AUROCH's strength is limitless, surging
from the shadowed earth;
an ancient bull bellows on the frozen moor –
but fine rain melts hard ice

ᚦ

3. THURS thrusting from the mindless rocks;
three thorns thrown for torment,
this force is terrible for man or woman to grasp.

ᚨ

4. ANSUZ is the tearing wind of Odhr's breath;
the mighty Word leads the wise,
but is a terrible sword to the common man

ᚱ

5. RIDING on the right road is a swift journey,
and in the hall a ready rede,
but rowning the rites is rough on the horse

⟨

6. KEN's cunning fire makes clear light;
yet children cannot play
with the scourge of art

✕

7. GIFT is honour to the host and good for the guest,
and a kiss that begets greatness;
though the wise should grasp the cost of the gain.

ᚹ

8. WYN is wonder when the wind waves the banner,
and happiness of the war-band;
but if a man lose his way in joyous company,
then woeful is his lot

ᚾ

9. HAIL is hurled from the heavens,
wreaking harm to crops, and havoc to the beast;
yet it is the seed of perfection,
sown for the world's remaking.

ᚩ

10. NEED is a narrow way through hardship,
and terrible toil;
yet it is a goad to greatness,
and the midwife of magic.

ᛁ

11. ICE is cold beauty, the bridge over endless chaos;
slippery and untrustworthy, it is death to the fey;
but the wise may use and enjoy, while trusting not.

⟨

12. YEAR brings to term whatever we sow;
the good earth guarantees growth -
but the gain is in grief
when the germ is rotten

13. YEW stands alone, strongest in the stead;
yet its branches bear berries of death;
and none but a Lord may string the bow of fire.

14. PERTHRO is played with passion and joy,
testing and igniting the luck of bold Lords;
yet things unknown to men are born in the web of Wyrd.

15. ELKSEDGE shoots up from the mud
sharp and dangerous to the young seeker
who tries to grasp it,
setting out on the bloody road to wisdom.

16. SUN's glory guides the seaman on his voyage;
if he has no love for clouds and ice,
victorious he returns

17. TYR the noble leader faces the great wolf;
a lone star shows him his truth;
often must he turn to guide his clan,
showing not his one hand.

ᛒ

18. BIRCH is first to brighten the young wood,
her lovely limbs beauty and birth and nurture;
but the unwary spirit may be lulled to sleep in her shade.

ᛗ

19. HORSE is true friend, good speed
among the nine worlds,
and joyous companionship;
but if carelessness brings nightmare,
then closeness is deadly

ᛉ

20. MAN is joy to man, glad mortal company
in the ship of forever;
but law and compromise must he make
when love fails

ᛚ

21. LAKE is life's water, and endless depth unto death,
and the place of fearful sacrifice;
but the leek thrusts up green and healing

◇

22. ING is the God of the old forest earth,
reaching East,
reversing the spin of the polar swastika,
bringing serpent gold from the ancient past.

ᛞ

23. DAY is the famous light,
mirth and hope to all,

and the unseen cleft in the world's dawn

ᛪ

24. HOME is the enclosure, warded with
inborn might, and holy,
where live the athelings in freedom and pleasure,
if there be right;
but many a stronghold is poor in spirit,
and a place of woe to its folks.

Chapter 13
Ginnung

From the pregnant gap, the zero of Ginnung, arises the primal dyad, fire and ice. Expansion in a puff of flame has a tendency to disperse instantly, and it is held in check by a tendency to condensation. This dynamic gives us forms such as atoms, titanic, ('giantish') fiery energies bounded in a tiny knot of spacetime.

From the heart of chaos, from the Gap at the core of what consciousness does, arises two kinds of inner work – magic and something else. This something else is often called meditation, and the word is useful, but likely to be misunderstood if I use that term without qualification. What I'm talking about here is the range of practices that cultivate the ability to double attention, to achieve ecstasis or transcendence.

This kind of work has suffered misunderstanding as a result of its names. Mystics would call it mysticism, but I think mysticism carries some very questionable ideological baggage. The term I favour is: a drive towards wholeness of experience. The attitude of the practitioner of this kind of work is one of acceptance of change and a basic faith in the benignity of the deep mind's processes. In Stanislav Grof's *holotropic breathwork*, which is a variety of connected breathwork, the attitude is of faith in the holotropic or wholeness-seeking function that Grof identifies as the basis of healing. The breathwork session is started lying down, with the hands open, symbolizing acceptance of what will come.

This is not a religious procedure. You don't have to believe in anything except the existence of part of you that is driven to call into you an improved way of experiencing the world, a new pattern that conditions your perception. The procedure is analogous to invoking something unknown, a new edition of your present self, from chaos or Ginnung, from the unmanifest processes of consciousness. It is a smaller scale version of Odin's sacrifice on Yggdrasil, in which he meets the Mystery, who gives him the runes. We aspire to a new assemblage of self, and the Mystery gives us the keys to our lives.

What are these new patterns, and where do they come from? I've called the source of these patterns 'chaos' or 'Ginnung'. Can we say more?

To some extent, the patterns are called in by specific aspirations. As a vehicle of aspiration, we may create an idealized self, a special magical self. This magical self, from one point of view, is an imagined thing. The creation of a magical self involves an act of imaginative aspiration, building an image of what we want to become.

Another type of aspirational self may not have such specific outlines, may partake more of chaos. Such a self is built of ecstatic consciousness, built of the sparks of total awareness that follow deconditioning. The identity has come adrift, but not in a psychotic way. Identity is merely suspended, not broken, while identification ceases. The attention is aware of the flow of events, but not choosing to identify, to make the usual internal monologue of self-identification. This self is hardly a self at all, in the sense of a cyclical, bounded trance. The arrow of its aspiration points to the unknown. This is about as near to a version of the Holy Guardian Angel as a metaphysical minimalist can accept.

That experience of flow replacing identity is valuable in itself. It refreshes deeply and may renew one's zest for life. What happens after that ecstasis is interesting too: identification with better patterns often results. The mundane selves will function better, and you will have an increased sense of self-possession, both in the mundane sense and in the sense that you no longer identify with selves without knowing you 'own' them.

New patterns have been taken up during ecstasis. Where do these new patterns originate? A Platonist would say the realm of Forms, eternal metaphysical ideal forms of all the categories of the perceived world. My own Holy Guardian Angel experiences seemed to indicate rather that they come from a kind of shadow-future which transmits information back in time, which seems to me no more incredible than Plato's dualistic metaphysics.

How we regard the source of the patterns may be a matter for personal taste. These notions don't require much theory, they are experiential realities. The method of practical aspiration is to aspire to the change and accept the transformation with the open-handed gesture of invoking the Mystery, Runa, to provide you with the keys to your life. Just as you learn to trust your intuition in magical action, you learn to trust the wholeness-seeking function of your mind to steer and sustain you as your present wholeness collapses into a higher coherence. That higher coherence emerges from Ginnung, chaos. Ginnung is not only that which makes magic possible, but also provides the reassortment of patterns that creates novelty.

It is worth noting that the results of the wholeness-seeking process are not dependent on conscious insights. Certainly, big, communicable insights can arise in the midst of breathwork or meditation, but many breathwork or meditation sessions end with no memorable insights. They usually end, however, with a distinct sense that things are better in some way. The point is that ecstasis is worthwhile in itself. The mechanism not only of the healing of sickness but of all positive self-readjustment may rely on a good dose of ecstasis.

The Ginnung Glyph

We can identify Fire with the wholeness-seeking process, the fluidity of selfhood, magic with Ice, the physicality of results.

Alternatively, we can identify Fire with magic, as the active, motive pole, and Ice with the wholeness-quest, for the stillness of the mind.

Like the Chinese dyad of yin and yang, this is not a fixed dualism, the categories changing and shifting as one thing changes into another.

The rune most closely referring to magical action, a *ansuz*, can be made into a pattern which resumes the entire dynamic of practical magic. The three *ansuz*es form a spinning vortex related to the triskele and the swastika:

ESC, 'GNOSIS'   BELIEF

DESIRE

The quest for wholeness can be glyphed by three t *tiwaz* runes. *Tiwaz* shows us an arrow pointing to the sky, the aspiration to cosmic order:

ASPIRATION

TRUST IN HOLOTROPIC   DOUBLING OF
PROCESS   AWARENESS

It is notable that the names of the two main runes in this glyph, *ansuz* and *tiwaz*, are both ancient words meaning 'god'. The rune ⌄ *ihwaz* is the hidden element of this process, the axis of transcendence or ecstasis itself, the line that runes from the surface of the earth to the Pole Star, the Nail round which the swastika of the Plough, Woden's Wain, revolves through the seasons.

The two diagrams can be combined into the single image of Ginnung, formed in and around the seed-crystal *hagalaz* form, mother of all the runestaves. In the original ice-crystal form, the expansive forces are in equilibrium with the contracting forces, and the hail-crystal is frozen. In the Ginnung glyph however we see how the dual powers of consciousness emerge from the seed. Each double-ended arrow carries its own dyad – ecstasy / ESCs, desire / aspiration, belief / trust – each a pair of facets of the same basic process. The whole glyph is enclosed in the circle of wholeness the *tiwaz* arrows aspire to.

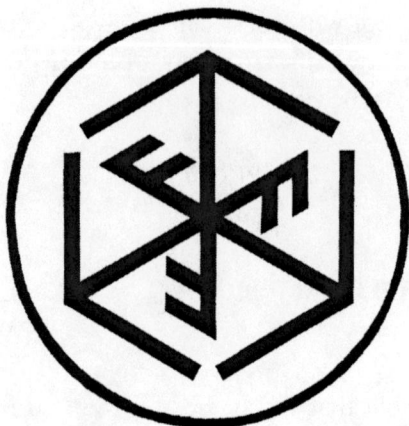

Ginnung

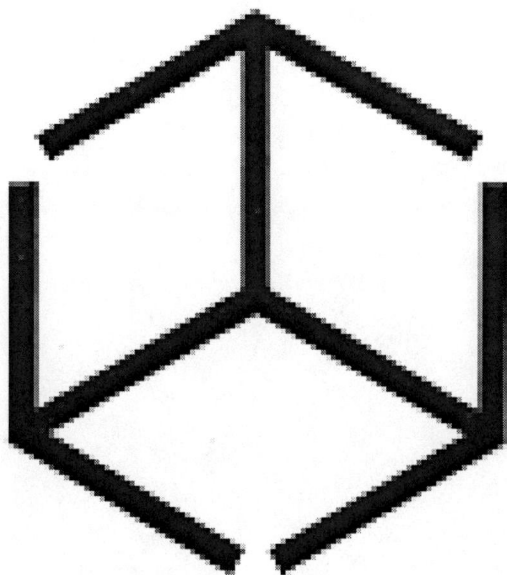

Appendix: Northern Myth Sources

This list is by no means exhaustive, merely a quick guide to some of the chief and most accessible sources used in this book.

The Poetic or Elder Edda

Völuspá Origins,	Gullveig/Heith, Ragnarok
Hávamál	Odhin's sacrifice
Vafthrudnism ál	the oldest Etins, the Ragnarok
Skirnismál	Frey and Gerdh
Lokasenna	Loki's final story
Rigsthula	story of Rig
Hindluljodh	Genealogy of gods
Short Seeress's Prophecy	Genealogy of gods including Heimdall

Recommended translations:
James Allen Chisholm's translation of the Eddas is excellent, and particularly useful to the magician – James Chisholm is a Master in the Rune Gild. The entire text is available free at: http://home.earthlink.net/~jordsvin/Norse%20Texts/The%20Eddas.htm

Lee M. Hollander's reissued classic translation is cast in resonant, archaic English to best capture the poetry of the originals. University of Texas Press, 1962, 1999.
The Prose Edda or Snorri's Edda

Gylfaginning
Origins, Odin, creation of Midgard, the first humans, Asgard and its fortifications, Yggdrasil, the Aesir, light Elves, Tyr and the binding of Fenriswolf, Frey and Skirnir, Valhalla, the Capture of Loki, the Ragnarok

Skaldskaparmal
Odin, Loki & Hoenir, Kvasir and the Mead

Heimskringla, by Snorri Sturluson
Ynglinga saga
Odin's brothers, the first War, Hoenir, Mimir, Kvasir, Freyja teaches Van magic to Aesir, Odhin's galdor and seith, Njordh

Recommended translation:
Lee M. Hollander, University of Texas Press, 1964, 1999.

Index

Mandrake

'Books you don't see everyday'

The Apophenion: A Chaos Magic Paradigm by Peter J Carroll.

978-1869928-421, £10.99

My final Magnum Opus if its ideas remain unfalsified within my lifetime, otherwise its back to the drawing board. Yet I've tried to keep it as short and simple as possible, it consists of eight fairly brief and terse chapters and five appendices.

It attacks most of the great questions of being, free will, consciousness, meaning, the nature of mind, and humanity's place in the cosmos, from a magical perspective. Some of the conclusions seem to challenge many of the deeply held assumptions that our culture has taught us, so brace yourself for the paradigm crash and look for the jewels revealed in the wreckage.
This book contains something to offend everyone; enough science to upset the magicians, enough magic to upset the scientists, and enough blasphemy to upset most trancendentalists.

The most original, and probably the most important, writer on Magick since Aleister Crowley.
-Robert Anton Wilson, author of the
Cosmic Trigger trilogy.

Magick Works: cutting edge essays from the path of Pleasure, Freedom and Power.
978-1869928-469 £10.99

Enter the world of the occultist: where the spirits of the dead dwell amongst us, where the politics of ecstasy are played out, and where magick spills into every aspect of life.

It's all right here; sex, drugs, witchcraft and gardening. From academic papers, through to first person accounts of high-octaine rituals. In Magick Works you will find cutting edge essays from the path of Pleasure, Freedom and Power.

In this seminal collection Julian Vayne explores;

* The Tantric use of Ketamine.
* Social Justice, Green Politics and Druidry.
* English Witchcraft and Macumba
* The Magickal use of Space.
* Cognitive Liberty and the Occult.
* Psychogeography & Chaos Magick.
* Tai Chi and Apocalyptic Paranoia.
* Self-identity, Extropianism and the Abyss.
* Parenthood as Spiritual Practice.
* Aleister Crowley as Shaman

CPSIA information can be obtained at www.ICGtesting.com
Printed in the USA
LVOW132032100412

276962LV00001B/37/P